G000241140

WATERLOOVILLE
A Pictorial History

Waterlooville town centre, 1985

WATERLOOVILLE
A Pictorial History

Barry Stapleton

Phillimore

1996

Published by
PHILLIMORE & CO. LTD.
Shopwyke Manor Barn, Chichester, West Sussex

© Barry Stapleton, 1996

ISBN 1 86077 08 8

Printed and bound in Great Britain by
BIDDLES LTD.
Guildford, Surrey

List of Illustrations

Frontispiece: Waterlooville town centre, 1985

Acknowledgements

One of the pleasures of writing a book on local history is meeting people who are not only keenly interested in the history of their community, but also are exceedingly generous in sharing their knowledge with a complete stranger. Waterlooville proved no exception and I am most grateful to many people for their help, including Mrs. Linda Wilson of Stakes Hill Road, Miss Grace Blackman, Miss Eileen Wadham, Mrs. Cissy Crooks, Mrs. Dodie Seaward, Bert Eames, Peter Faulkner of Waterlooville F.C., Arthur Weston for information about Osmond and Osmond, Katie Hunt of Westerly and Freddie Thompson of Inchcape Motors Retail for information about Wadham Brothers. In particular, however, I am very pleased to acknowledge Tony Edwards of the building company Edwards & Son, not only for much personal assistance, but also for allowing me access to the company's books from which otherwise unavailable information was gleaned.

In addition my former colleagues at the University of Portsmouth: Dr. John Chapman, Dr. James Thomas, Antonio da Cruz and Roger Homer provided information and help in a number of ways. Gavin Maidment of Havant Museum allowed access to their photographic collection as did Philippa Stevens at the Local Studies Library, Winchester. The majority of the photographs in this book, however, come from the Marshall Collection housed at the Hampshire County Museum Service, Bar End, Winchester. There can be fewer friendlier or pleasant places in which to undertake research; staff were always helpful and I am particularly grateful to Alastair Penfold for considerable assistance. In this context, it is most appropriate that both the author and the publishers express their deep appreciation to Philip H. Marshall for permission to use the Marshall collection and the Hampshire Museums Service for granting access and providing facilities for its perusal. There is no doubt that without the benefit of Herbert Marshall's evocative photography, not only would this book have been the poorer, but it could not have been produced at all. Waterlooville owes its pioneering photographer a lasting debt of gratitude.

Similarly, I have benefited from the help provided by the staff at the Hampshire County Record Office, Portsmouth City Record Office and Portsmouth Central Library. Most of all, however, I have to thank Geoff Salter, Deputy Divisional Librarian, at Waterlooville who was most willing to share with me his considerable knowledge about the community and its history. I hope Geoff, in particular, but also all others who have given their assistance feel that their efforts have been rewarded with a worthwhile publication.

At Phillimore, Nicola Willmot and Christine Hanson provided advice with patience to one who, I suspect, was not the easiest of their authors. Lastly, my thanks to Mary Banks, who typed the manuscript not only skilfully but with great good humour and still remains a friend!

For any remaining errors I alone am responsible.

Gratitude is expressed, for permission to publish illustrations, to the following; Grace Blackman, 58, 114, 121, 134, 142; Mrs. Cissie Crook, 124, 125; Miss Eileen Wadham, 25, 76, 77; Bert Beames, 2, 9, 11, 12, 14, 15, 16, 18, 46, 47, 103, 126; Tony Edwards, 67, 68; Hampshire Local Studies Collection, County Library, Winchester, 70; Havant Museum, 88, 111, 123; *The News*, Portsmouth, frontispiece, 45; South-East Divisional Library, Waterlooville, 10, 13, 19-21, 26, 32, 35-37, 42, 44, 49, 52, 56, 65, 72-75, 79-81, 83, 102, 128-32, 143, 145, 146; Waterlooville Football Club, 139-41; Hampshire Museums Service and Philip H. Marshall for the remainder from the Marshall Collection. The advertisements are from the *William's Guide*.

Maps, 1, 4, 5 and 6 are reproduced from Ordnance Survey and are: Map 1, 1810, 1" = 1mile; Map 4, 1895, 6" = 1 mile; Map 5, 1933, 6" = 1 mile; Map 6, 1939, 25" = 1 mile. Copies of maps 1, 4 and 6 were provided by Portsmouth City Records Office and map 5 by the Map Library, University of Portsmouth. Map 2 the Bere Forest Enclosure, 1812 and Map 3 Farlington Parish Tithe Map, 1838, were supplied by Hampshire Record Office. Grateful thanks are expressed to all.

To Sandie
for everything

Waterlooville—Origins and Development

Unlike most of its surrounding communities, Waterlooville has no long history. Whereas contiguous parishes such as Farlington, Catherington, Southwick and Hambledon were all long established communities, even containing ancient villages such as Horndean in Catherington parish and Purbrook in Farlington parish, Waterlooville did not even exist until after the beginning of the 19th century. It is thus less than two centuries old yet is now larger in population size than all its neighbours. For the historian this has its disadvantages as well as advantages. On the one hand it is not possible to write a lengthy history of the growth and development of a community from ancient or medieval times to the present day. On the other hand with such a short time span to cover, it is much more likely that records will have survived to illuminate its history or otherwise become available because they were simply the product of modern times.

By the time Waterlooville began to be established Britain was already well into its Industrial Revolution and on the verge of the age of steam with railways and ships revolutionising transport, as steam-powered spindles had already revolutionised the textile industries and steam-powered threshing machines made inroads into agriculture.

Large cities had emerged in the industrial north and Midlands; Manchester, Liverpool, Leeds, Sheffield, Newcastle and Birmingham were already major centres of industry and commerce before Waterlooville had even begun. Few communities, apart from deliberately planted ones, such as the new towns of the 19th century, like New Lanark and Saltaire, owing much to individual founders, and those of the 20th, resulting from local and national planning like Letchworth or Milton Keynes, have such recent origins and it is the purpose of this book to indicate when and how Waterlooville began, to show what sort of people came to live there and the type of community which emerged, as well as to examine its growth and expansion in the 20th century.

In the late 17th century travellers from London to Portsmouth would invariably halt at Horndean for refreshment, and possibly a change of horses, at one of the inns such as the *Ship and Bell* or *Red Lion*. They would then continue their journey either by the track which led through the Forest of Bere to Purbrook and Cosham or, the more prudent would eschew the long stretch of unbroken forest land and travel via Rowlands Castle to Havant, turn west along the coast through Bedhampton and Farlington to Cosham, and thence to Portsmouth.

From the late 17th century, however, Portsmouth expanded rapidly, for its dock-yard became of growing importance as a major naval base. One consequence was the establishment of a Turnpike Trust in 1710, formed to improve the southern end of the direct route from London by creating a turnpike road between Portsmouth and Sheet Bridge, north of Petersfield. Shortly after the first meeting of the Trust, in June 1711, travellers along the road would be expected to pay at tollbooths on Portsbridge and Sheet Bridge and in return the Turnpike Trust would use the income received to repair

Map 1 The London Road and Forest of Bere, 1810.

the road to a reasonable standard. It seems likely that the road surface was improved, since not only was there an increase in the number of through coaches, but also the journey times were shortened. What had been an arduous trek of some sixteen hours in the 1770s had been reduced to nine or ten hours by 1805.

Even so, as the first Ordnance Survey map of England shows (*see* map 1), the stretch of road from Horndean to Purbrook remained devoid of habitation except for a single farmhouse at Wait Lane End (Wheat Lane End). For most of that distance the road passed through the outlying parts of the parishes of Catherington and Farlington and some of the densest stretches of the Forest of Bere. Part of the forest road traversed an area which was outside the jurisdiction of any parish—what was termed an extra-parochial area, one in which no parish authority was responsible for the upkeep of the road.

In medieval times the Forest of Bere became one of the Royal Forests and covered much of southern Hampshire from Southampton in the west to the Sussex border in the east. By the beginning of the 19th century there were about 16,000 acres of the forest still surviving in two areas, the West Walk near Wickham and the East Walk, which surrounded much of the road from Horndean to Purbrook. The lack of population along this road, however, not only represented the fact of royal ownership, but also that the soil was impermeable clay, an intractable surface which was infertile, did not hold water, was unsuitable for cereal growing, but capable of supporting trees which could grow to considerable heights. Thus, infertile and lacking a water supply, the area remained generally uninhabited.

The catalyst for growth and development of the area was the Enclosure of the Forest of Bere. In 1810 an Act of Parliament was passed approving the enclosure of about 8,000 acres, thus creating areas of private ownership within what had been open forest. But enclosure was costly. Commissioners, appointed to carry out the enclosure and to see that all were treated fairly, had to be paid and a new infrastructure of roads had to be laid down so that access to individual holdings could be obtained. Thus, a number of 'Public Carriage Roads and Highways over the Forest of the width of thirty feet' were specified, and included one 'Road called Hambledon and Stakes Hill Road beginning at Barn Green [now Denmead] Lane, and leading south-eastward along the present gravel road, to and over the London and Portsmouth Turnpike Road commonly called the London Road and over the Forest to and over Stakes Hill'. The 'present gravel road' can be seen to join the London Road near Wait Lane End Farm, and thence to Stakes, an already well-established hamlet long before Waterlooville existed (*see* map 1). However, the new road was to form a crossroads with the London road and create a new direct road to Stakes (*see* map 2). This new crossroads was to become the centre of Waterlooville but was clearly an empty space in 1810. The only buildings in the vicinity were Farlington Workhouse for the poor, established on the northern parish boundary, as far away from the village of Farlington as possible, Wheat (Wait) Lane End Farm (off map 2 to the south-west along the London Road), and the collection of long buildings which, subsequently, turn out to be those of a brickworks with probably a row of labourers' cottages on the opposite side of the road.

The land in the northern quadrant of the crossroads, between the Hambledon and London roads, was to be sold by the Commissioners to defray the expenses of enclosure and was bought up mainly by men from Portsmouth. Thomas Fitzherbert, Esq. of Stubbington Manor, Portsmouth, a wealthy farmer, bought the two lots which fronted both the Hambledon and London roads. James Smith, gentleman, of Baffins Farm, Portsea bought the next allotment along the London road, followed by William Ellis the elder, gentleman, of Portsea who acquired the fourth and sixth allotments on either side of that of James White, gentleman, of Purbrook. Then came an allotment for building a chapel in the Forest. Allotments in both the western and southern quadrants went largely to Charles William Taylor, but the eastern quadrant was divided into much smaller plots and especially so on the south-eastern side of Stakes Hill Road.

Fitzherbert, Smith, Ellis and White all purchased their allotments in 1810 and shortly afterwards advertisements began to appear in the Hampshire newspapers for plots of land for sale with a view to developing villas on the sites. Probably the first development came on Fitzherbert's corner allotment for in 1814 he sold the over three acres plot to a Mr. Charles Mathews who proceeded to have an inn built on the site sometime between February 1814 when, according to the title deeds, the land was sold, and September 1824, when the *Heroes of Waterloo Inn* was mortgaged by Mathews to a Mr. John Burrill.

From then until 1838 some slow and steady development occurred in the vicinity of the crossroads, mainly in the western quadrant along the London and Hambledon roads and on the north-eastern side of Stakes Hill Road (*see* map 3). Both the southern and eastern corners of the crossroads remained undeveloped, as did the northern quadrant beyond the *Heroes of Waterloo Inn*. Unfortunately, map 3 does not cover all of what was to be Waterlooville since it is the tithe map of Farlington parish and was

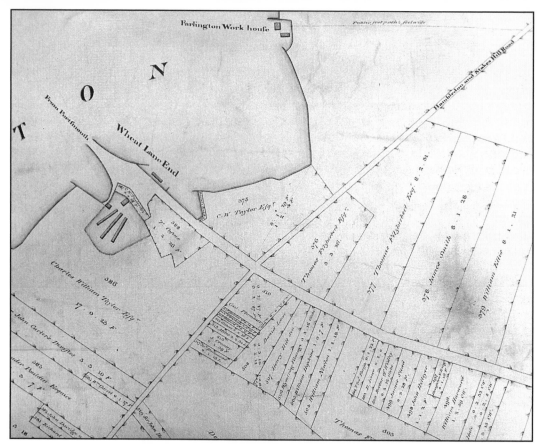

Map II   Forest of Bere enclosure creates the crossroads, 1812.

not concerned with those areas outside its jurisdiction. Thus, it shows the parish boundary passing through the centre of the crossroads created in 1810. What lay to the north and east of that boundary was the extra-parochial area which was left blank except for the *Waterloo* building on the corner i.e. the *Heroes of Waterloo Inn*. The community which had grown was given the name of Wheat Lane End, after the existing farm, as it had been called on the Enclosure and Tithe maps (maps 2 and 3).

However, in November 1828, ten years before the Tithe map had been produced, some of the inhabitants of the settlement established a committee which was to take the necessary steps for the erection of a church or chapel to accommodate the inhabitants of the extra-parochial places, as well as those on the borders of the parishes of Hambledon, Catherington, Southwick, Farlington, Wymering, Widley, Blendworth and Bedhampton, estimated to be a population of 1,100. The Enclosure Commissioners had been required to set apart 10 acres, the rents of which had to be invested and applied to the expense of building any chapel which may be erected and the inhabitants had, by voluntary subscription, plus a sum from the Incorporated Society for Promoting Churches 'caused a Chapel to be built on a site on the Extra parochial Land situated near a place called Wheat Lane End'. The site was to be on the north-western side of the Hambledon Road (not the London Road site allocated by the Enclosure Commissioners). The chapel was consecrated for public worship on 26 January 1831. The Act of Consecration referred to it as St George's Chapel, Waterloo—thus creating a distinction between the name of that part of the community established in the extra-

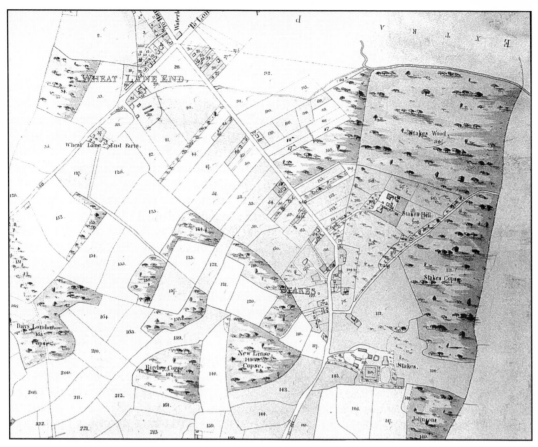

Map III Wait Lane End, Farlington parish, 1838.

parochial area and that in Farlington parish—namely Wait Lane (or Wheat Lane) End. Of the six named petitioners in the Act of Consecration three, Daniel Hewitt, William Friend and William Gauntlett, had land and property at Wait Lane End and a fourth was John Spice Hulbert of Stakes Hill Lodge.

The Farlington Tithe Award provides detail of the owners and occupiers of the land in Farlington parish. On the corner of Hambledon Road opposite the *Heroes* was a grocer's shop rented by Edward Yeulett, and next door to him on the London Road was farmer, Thomas Drewett. Two doors from Drewett was general dealer, William Kennett and next to him butcher, Richard Loveder. In what was to become Chapel Lane, was baker, Jane Gard. On the east side of Stakes Hill Road were shoemaker, Isaac Hayward; tailor, Samuel Fox; dealer, John Brazier and in the last house farmer, John Hayward. Thus it can be seen that a thriving small community was being established, no doubt assisted by the growing volume of passing traffic—by 1835 there were 16 coaches daily from London to Portsmouth and increasingly the *Heroes Inn* was a stopping place, and neighbouring shops would benefit. The growing number of houses would have been helped by the existence of two brickyards in Wait Lane End, the smaller one was on the northern parish boundary, owned and occupied by William Bellingham and the larger (which was also on the Enclosure Map, map 2) was owned by John Spice Hulbert and, no doubt, produced most of the bricks needed after growth began from 1814. On the main road, just south of the brickyard, between it and Wheat Lane End Farm, lived Henry Greast, the village blacksmith. Other residents tended to be agricultural labourers, indicating the basically rural nature of the community. In fact, because land use is indicated on the tithe award, it is possible to determine the amount of farmland in the community. There were something approaching fifty acres of pastureland and thirty acres of arable in the Farlington parish area alone. Woodland had been reduced to just over seven acres, whereas Stakes was still surrounded by much woodland and the extra-parochial area also was dominated by forest.

From 1841 it is possible to get a more complete picture of development since, for the first time, the extra-parochial area called Waterloo was given a population total in the census. The censuses of Great Britain were taken every ten years from 1801, but few, if any, of the original enumerators' returns survive before 1841, only the outline figures for each parish. However, a note about Farlington parish in the 1821 census states, 'the increase of Population is ascribed to the inclosure of the Forest of Bere', thus supporting the view that enclosure was the agent of change. Ten years later, the census noted that the return for the Parish of Farlington 'includes the population of much Extra Parochial Land, part of the late Forest of Bere whereon several houses are built, and recently a small chapel'. The latter is clearly a reference to St George's, Waterloo. Thus, the census notes indicate something of the early development of Waterlooville, and are confirmed by the Tithe Map of 1838 (map 3). However, it has been usual in 20th-century publications for the population of the extra-parochial area to be given as that for Waterloo as a whole, indicating that the part of Waterloo called Wait Lane End (or Wheat Lane End) had been recorded in the census as part of the population of Farlington parish. Strictly speaking this is true, but these two settlements were part of what was a single expanding community. Thus an attempt is made here to assess the real population of the joint communities.

Table 1

Census Population 1841-1891

	Waterloo	Farlington Parish (Wait Lane End estimate)	Total	Stakes	Overall Total
1841	175	180	355	144	499
1851	195	205	381	127	508
1861	243	269	511	147	658
1871	283	425?	708	204?	912
1881	246?	436	682	151	833
1891	436	564	918	187	1105

This exercise is fraught with difficulties since no postal addresses were given in the censuses, only the names of roads in which houses were located. Additionally, census enumerators did not always progress logically from house to house and did not always get the street names right; for example, Stakes Hill Road was often given as Stakes Road, thus potentially confusing it with the road of the same name at Purbrook. Consequently, it is not always easy to know whether the division was made between where Wait Lane End houses ended and those of Stakes began. Thus, the bulge in population in 1871 looks suspiciously high, particularly the Stakes population of 204

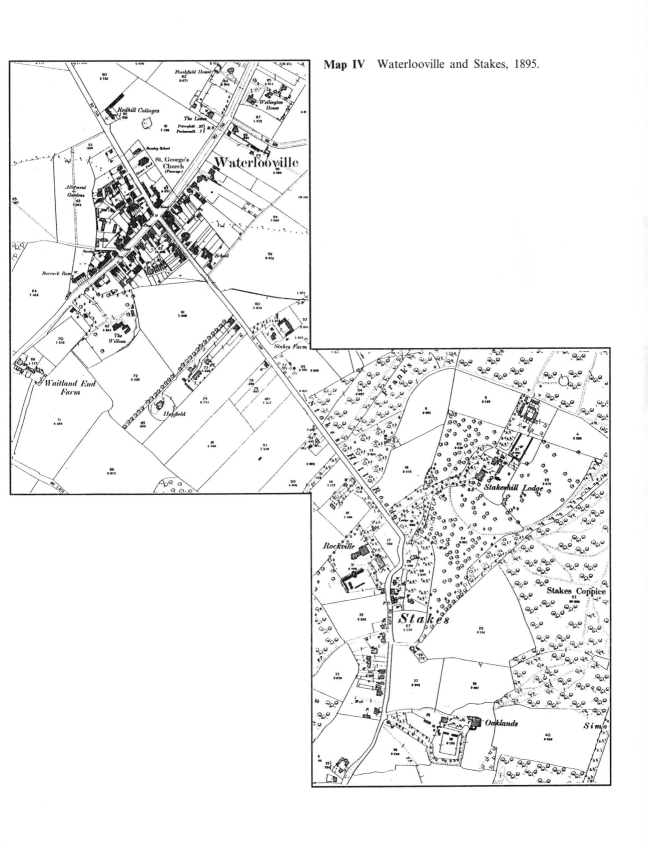

Map IV Waterlooville and Stakes, 1895.

and the Wait Lane estimate of 425. Similarly, the Waterloo population of 246 in 1881 looks too low. Even so, bearing these problems in mind, what is clear is that while the population of Stakes, a long established community, grew only gradually (30 per cent in 50 years), that of Wait Lane End/Waterloo, developed only since about 1815, grew quickly, and had eclipsed the population of Stakes in under twenty-five years. Its location on the main London-Portsmouth road was, naturally, a prime reason for this growth, as well as the fact that population in England as a whole was growing—it doubled from nine million to 18 million between 1801 and 1851. After that its growth slowed (1891: 27 million—an increase of 50 per cent) whilst that of Waterloo and Wait Lane End did not, almost trebling between 1841 and 1891, with the number of occupied houses rising from 69 to 146, whilst in Stakes they increased from 30 to only 37.

The growth of the community at Waterloo is also implied by the returns of the religious census of 1851 in which St George's Chapel was said to have a congregation of about three hundred and fifty people at its morning service and to have sittings for five hundred. Such attendances, no doubt, influenced the Anglican authorities, since a new parish of Waterloo was established a few years later in 1858.

From 1841 it is possible to discover something about the community growing up around the crossroads, and what is clear is that agricultural labour dominated men's occupations and domestic service that of women. In 1841, 54 agricultural labourers were listed in the census and two general labourers. Female domestic servants numbered 35 plus two charwomen, three laundresses, a domestic nurse and a housekeeper—42 in all. In addition there were 16 male domestic servants. However, all these workers were unevenly distributed; Wait Lane End and extra-parochial Waterloo had more agricultural labourers than Stakes, which was in a generally wooded area. However, Stakes and Waterloo had many more of the domestic servants than Wait Lane End. Both contained more people who were financially independent—14 in Stakes, 10 in Waterloo, but only four in Wait Lane End. Thus, Stakes was already an area which attracted people with wealth, like John Hulbert who, around the beginning of the 19th century, bought Stakes Hill Cottage (now 71 Stakes Hill Road) and then proceeded to expand his land ownership, building Stakes Hill Lodge (as a summer residence) in 1820, and by 1838 owning over 350 acres. The Taylor family, living at Oaklands, were also considerable landowners in Stakes and Wait Lane End (*see* maps 2 and 3). In the extra-parochial area of Waterloo the independent residents included John Billett of Highfield Lodge and William Gauntlett of Hambledon Road. Wait Lane End, by contrast, tended to be dominated by people in trade. Here were the shops: the baker, the butcher and general stores, with the grocer's shop on the corner of Hambledon Road and London Road, its garden in Wait Lane End in the parish of Farlington and the shop in extra-parochial Waterloo. The *Heroes of Waterloo* was across the Hambledon Road. The craftsmen also tended to concentrate in Wait Lane End—a blacksmith, a carpenter and a shoemaker, tailors and bricklayers were all resident here. But the overwhelming impression is of a small rural community which was dominated by farming.

Ten years later the pattern tended to be much the same with an increase in agricultural labourers to 62, female domestic servants reaching 40 and laundresses quadrupling to twelve. Increasing numbers of servants suggest rising numbers of wealthy residents and indeed there was the beginning of middle-class professions—with an auctioneer, two teachers—one a professor of music—and a couple of clerks being resident. Perhaps the most significant development was the appearance of a number of retired people—six in Waterloo and one in Stakes. Clearly the wooded area of the Forest of Bere had its attractions for those wishing to escape both work and the urban environment. Men such as Thomas White and Benjamin Elliott, both aged 56, retired from Portsea Island. Not surprisingly, shops continued to increase, including a draper's, an additional baker's and four grocers' shops—two in Wait Lane End and two in Waterloo. James Restall, grocer and baker, aged 27, was at the first residence named in Stakes Hill Road. The existence of these additional shops is the strongest evidence that the southern and eastern corners of the crossroads must have begun to be developed during the 1840s. The presence of a coach builder in Waterloo indicated the growth of a luxury trade for the wealthy and the increase in bricklayers from two to eight, as well as the arrival of two painters and glaziers and a plumber, plus a doubling in the number of carpenters, indicated the expansion of the building industry as the community grew. A name which was to become significant in the development of Waterlooville first appeared in the 1851 census when 17-year-old John Edwards, founder of Waterlooville's oldest existing business, appeared as an apprentice bricklayer living in his brother's house. The first reference to a miller also indicated the existence of a Waterlooville windmill, on Mill Hill.

But the growth of a community along a main road from Portsmouth to the capital could no doubt bring its problems, as another occupation making its first appearance in 1851 was that of a police constable, perhaps partly required by the appearance of a second inn, the *Belle Alliance*, on the northern corner of Chapel Lane. Whilst the Hulberts continued at Stakes Hill Lodge, Oaklands was unoccupied in 1851—no doubt because William Taylor, aged 75 in 1841, had subsequently died. Four years later the house was in the hands of Lady Napier and was to remain in the Napier family's possession for over fifty years.

It seems likely that the name Waterlooville originated in the parish register, which begins in 1832 with a baptism in Waterloo. However, in August 1834 the community was described as 'Waterloo Ville extra parochial' and remained as such until November 1855, when it reverted to Waterloo. Then, in the 1851 census, Waterloo was not described like all other communities in Hampshire, as a parish, town, tything, chapelry or extra-parochial area, but as a *ville*. A note in the census states 'The Parish of Farlington, with the Area of which that of Waterloo Ville is returned ...' officially confirmed the name. Certainly in 1855 the *Post Office Directory* of Hampshire refers to Waterlooville with Stakes although White's *Directory* 1859 has the hyphenated form—Waterloo-Ville.

The mid-1850s also saw the beginning of Nonconformist worship in Waterlooville with Baptists and Congregationalists meeting from 1854, presumably in a building designated a chapel, since the 1855 *Directory* refers to it. However, the first real Baptist Chapel was erected in 1856 and opened in May that year. Two years later Waterlooville was designated an Anglican parish of 652 acres. A decade afterwards, a Sunday school building was erected by Edwards for £147 10s. and opened on 10 March 1869. There were 140 children present, it being the only public education provided in the village. By the mid-1850s it also had its own postal service; William Yeulett, at the grocer's shop on the western corner of the crossroads being postmaster in 1855. But by 1859, though Yeulett was still there, the post office had crossed to James Restall's grocery shop in Stakes Hill Road. Horse buses ran from Portsmouth to Petersfield

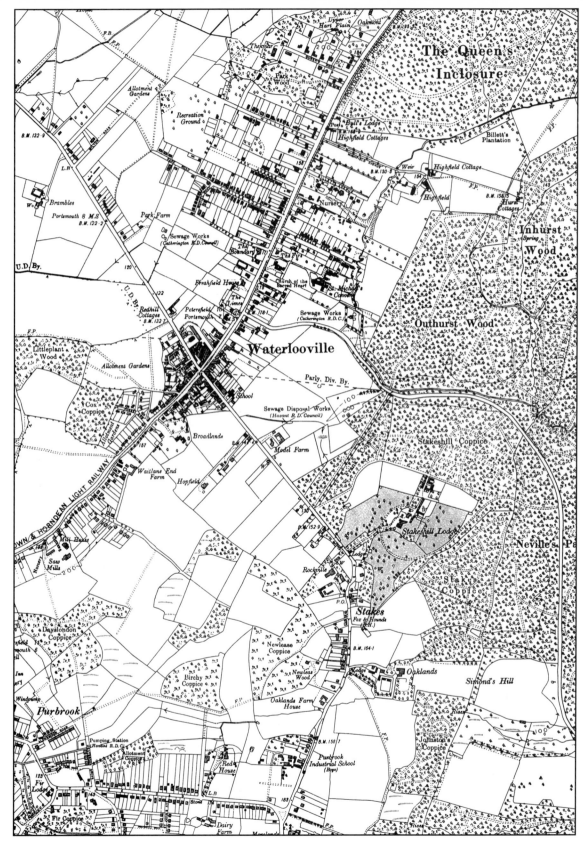

Map V   Waterlooville and Stakes, 1933.

through the village and stopped at the *Waterloo Inn*, as it had begun to be called rather than the *Heroes of Waterloo*, as it had been named in the title deeds until 1856. When it was bought by Richard Gale of the Horndean Brewery in 1860 it had already become the *Waterloo Inn.* The original old inn was a long, rambling building which, with its stables, stretched from the churchyard in Hambledon Road around the corner to the meadow in London Road. Freight carrying services were provided to Portsmouth from Hambledon and Horndean. Thus, the speed of travel was restricted to that of the horse, at least until arriving at Cosham station three miles away.

Even so, one fascinating aspect of Waterlooville in the mid-1850s was that it possessed two lodging houses, both located in Stakes Hill Road. George Webb had the first at what was to become, by 1859, the *Bricklayer's Arms*, and the other was the house of Isaac Hayward who was a shoemaker. It seems that Waterlooville's population was either growing too fast for its housing, or was exhibiting the beginnings of its attraction for visitors and, perhaps in recognition of this, the 1861 census indicates the presence, for the first time, of the *Wellington Inn*. Though unoccupied when the census was taken, by 1867 John Redford was the innkeeper. By that time the village had its own carriers— the Silvesters of Stakes who advertised a daily service to Portsmouth.

As the community continued to grow, so did the number of agricultural labourers. Employed on seven farms, they reached a peak of 70 in 1871 with a number of them living in the newly-developed Swiss Road. Domestic servants also continued to increase, some 62 females being employed along with 20 laundresses, eight cooks, six domestic nurses and six housekeepers. Male servants became more specialised—22 gardeners, six coachmen and eight grooms, plus two butlers represented a move from general to specific duties for men, an indication of the continued expansion of the numbers of well-to-do. Such growth in a literate sector of the population no doubt led to a change at James Restall's post office from 1871. What had been only one collection and delivery per day was changed to two and, whereas postal and money orders had been available previously from Horndean, Havant or Cosham, they could now be issued and paid in Waterlooville. Before the 1870s were over it was said that 'spring, summer and autumn, Waterloo is filled with visitors from Portsmouth, Southsea etc., who are attracted by the well-known purity of the air' (White's *History Gazetteer* and *Directory of Hampshire*, 1878). Not only was the air pure but Kelly's *Directory* of 1880 added that it was 'particularly suitable for those who require a more bracing atmosphere and yet one that is adapted to weak chests'. Not surprisingly, therefore, the 1881 census shows not only one hotel keeper but also four boarding house keepers. By the beginning of the 20th century both had doubled in number, with the *Queen's Hotel* having replaced the *Belle Alliance* by the late 1880s.

A name which was to become well-known not only in Waterlooville, but also throughout southern England, first appeared in the 1871 census, when Charles Wadham from Cowes on the Isle of Wight, and Edwin Stent had a partnership (established in 1868) in a draper's shop in Victoria House, London Road. Even then, the corner of London Road and Stakes Hill Road, where Wadham's was later to develop (now the site of Lloyds Bank), was still a garden. Ten years later Stent was not to be found in Waterlooville and Wadham, then a draper, outfitter and hatter, was married with four children. He had also been joined by two other Wadhams from the Isle of Wight both of whom lived in Stakes Hill Road. George Wadham ran a daily carrying service to Portsmouth and had done so from at least 1878, but 30-year-old Henry Wadham, married with three sons and a daughter, was said to be a draper. By 1885 Charles Wadham had moved his shop to The Exchange and it would appear that Henry was an assistant there, as he was described as a draper's assistant in 1891 when he had five sons between the ages of four and fourteen and two daughters. By then Charles Wadham had three sons and three daughters, and by the mid-1890s had added boot and shoe maker, milliner and dressmaker, tricycle agent, funeral furnisher and agent for the Brunswick Steam Dyeing and Carpet Beating Company to his drapery and outfitter's business. Curiously, however, it was not his family but Henry's which was to continue the business, Charles Wadham's name having disappeared by the early 20th century to be replaced by Henry's as operating the drapery store, and Henry's three sons, Astley, Percy and Stanley were to grow up and run the business for many years. However, it was the other two sons who were to make the Wadham name famous, Harold beginning a cycle business in Stakes Hill Road in 1900 from which, when later joined by his younger brother, Wilfred, the Wadham Brothers' Motor Company was to grow into Waterlooville's biggest employer.

Opposite Wadham's cycle business in Stakes Hill Road was James Restall's grocery and baker's shop which he had run since the 1850s (along with being the postmaster) and which his youngest son Lacey took over around 1910, although without the post office. Restall's nephew, George Pook, who had been an assistant in the grocery shop, took over as postmaster as well as being a printer and stationer, on the corner of Hambledon Road opposite the *Heroes*.

In keeping with Waterlooville's rising status as a visitor centre, it began to expand. In the 1870s came Chapel Lane and the establishment of a School Board in 1876, which rented the old village school pending the opening of a new Board School for 160 children, which took place in Stakes Hill Road in 1880, the foundation stone being laid in 1879.

The 1880s saw the building of the new Baptist Chapel with funds provided by George Lancaster and his father John. It had an imposing Italianate frontage, creating the most striking architectural feature of the London Road. The same decade the Hulbert Road, opened in 1881 after four years in the making and paid for entirely by George Hulbert, created a new direct route to Bedhampton (*see* map 4 for these developments).

In 1880 came the Victoria Hall on the north side of Stakes Hill Road, built for concerts and entertainment and containing a Ladies Club by the turn of the century. A Waterloo Parish Reading Room had also been erected by Edwards & Son for the princely sum of £184 18s. 8d. But these public buildings were only one aspect of progress. There also needed to be public services. Thus the Portsmouth Water Works Company supplied piped water in the late 19th century. Gas was also piped and a new and second sewage works was added in 1898—necessary because the original in Farlington parish did not cater for growth in the new Waterloo parish, which was in the Catherington Union and not the Havant Union to which Farlington belonged. Similarly, new pavements were laid in the 1890s. Over one hundred and fifty yards were completed in 1896 in Wait Lane End to be followed by fifty yards more in 1899 and over one hundred and sixty yards at Stakes. Not surprisingly, Catherington Rural District Council felt the need to follow suit and laid over sixty yards of pavement on the west side of Hambledon Road. The west side of London Road, north from the *Heroes*, remained unpaved, since this was the location for the old Waterloo Fair.

Meanwhile, the Catherington Council had been busily getting Edwards & Son to install street lighting, putting a lamp standard in Beaconsfield Road in 1897, two in Avondale Road the following year and one in each of Jubilee and Muriel Roads (1899 and 1901 respectively). These were oil lamps, as had been others supplied by Havant Rural District Council, and a lamplighter had to be employed, with oil supplied by Timothy Whites. The first lamp was erected outside Charles Wadham's shop at the crossroads and was the only one for some time. Modernisation, however, arrived in the early 20th century with the establishment by 1905 of a public call office by the National Telephone Company. In 1898 the fire brigade's existence was indicated by the installation of an alarm bell by Edwards. No doubt this development was a direct result of the events one late May night in 1895 when the *Hampshire Telegraph* of 1 June 1895 reported:

A serious fire, which resulted in several thousands of pounds' worth of damage, occurred on Tuesday night at Waterlooville, near Portsmouth.

It appears that shortly before eleven o' clock one of the men in the employ of Mr. Pennekett, baker and grocer, heard the cracking and falling of slates. He immediately investigated the matter, and found that the back portion of the premises was on fire. Mr. Pennekett sen., and his son were away, but Mrs. Pennekett and her child were in bed. They were aroused, and made a hurried exit into the street. The fire appeared to be of considerable extent, and the whole village soon turned out, everyone being thoroughly alarmed. There are no fire appliances in the village, though a fire-engine of some sort has been long felt to be a necessity. Mr. Restall, therefore, undertook to go to Havant on a bicycle, and did so, giving the alarm to the brigade, which at once turned out. He occupied a considerable time in accomplishing the journey, owing to the bad stony state of the roads. A second messenger followed in a trap and took back the captain of the brigade, Mr. Stent, with a hose, which was at once attached to a hydrant, a good supply of water being thus delivered on to the fire.

The flames had spread rapidly, and had taken a good hold of the back of Mr. Pennekett's premises and extended to the adjoining buildings. The whole of the people in the village watched the progress of the flames with anxiety. Mr. Wadham, who lives in the Exchange, next door to Pennekett's, got his family into the street, but was reassured on finding that the wind blew away from his shop. Mrs. Pennekett and the child were taken in by Mr. Wadham and given shelter. It was not very long before the shop of Mr. Long, butcher, which adjoins Pennekett's, was ablaze, and the dwelling house of Mrs. Carter also caught.

SAD DOMESTIC LOSSES
The Havant Fire Brigade arrived shortly before twelve o'clock, and at once got to work. Their efforts prevented the fire spreading, but it looked so likely that other houses would catch that several people moved their portable goods into the street. The roof of Mr. Pennekett's shop gradually burst through and collapsed, and when the fire was finally got under, after two hours' hard work, three buildings involved were completely burnt out, almost every article of stock at Mr. Pennekett's was destroyed, but the books and cash-box were saved. Mrs. Long lost absolutely everything, including every article of her wardrobe except the dressing gown in which she escaped into the street, and she had to be supplied with clothing by the neighbours. In the shop only a lamb chop was left. Not even the vestige of a chair or table was to be found.

The property belongs to Mr. G.S. Lancaster, J.P., and is insured. At present the exact cause of the outbreak is unknown, but it is supposed that some straw was ignited by wood ashes.

Clearly, had Waterlooville had its own brigade, the fire could have been contained earlier and less damage caused. That the burnt-out properties were owned by George Lancaster of Melton House was no real surprise, since he seemed to be the largest local property owner, having some forty to fifty buildings in the centre of Waterlooville. Photographic evidence shows that new buildings soon replaced those burnt down, and patently it was considered that no repeat of the fire should occur for, by 1907 and probably earlier, there was a fire brigade, which by 1910 was well organised consisting of a captain and eight men, all thoroughly trained and efficient, the appliances kept at the rear of the *Heroes of Waterloo* hotel.

However, at the turn of the century Waterlooville was still a small village with a number of shops, two hotels, a chalk and flint main road with picturesque beech and chestnut trees overhanging and mainly horse-drawn traffic, including the three-in-hand horse buses which ran every hour from Cosham to the *Waterloo Hotel*, behind which they had their stables. The buses were operated by Alfred W. White, but by the end of 1901 the bus stables were in the hands of White's Provincial Tramway Company Ltd. which had sold its Portsmouth trams to the City Corporation.

The bus services were not solely for residents but also for visitors. The attractions for them included, as *William's Guide* stated:

> woods and forests; green fields and waving fields of grain; beautiful gardens and parks; stately houses and pretty country villas; ... comfortable and economical places for rest and refreshment, whilst in the country around there are scores of delightful walks and rambles, midst an air that is redolent of pines and wild flowers, and of a highly bracing character.

All the visitors had to be provided with services, as had the growing number of retired and wealthy residents, hence, the large number of domestic servants. For many of the servants, however, life was somewhat impoverished. Whilst Stakes Hill Lodge had its water closets for the Hulbert family, in 1895 Edwards were asked, by John Hulbert, to fit up servants' earth closets, and Edith Blackman (née Miles) described her time as a servant with the Learmonths at Rockville, Stakes (*see* map 4) as very hard:

> A very hard place because there was such a lot of it. Oh the old grates used to have to be polished, the drawing room done and the grate was all steel and brass. We always rubbed over two fireplaces in the drawing room because it was such a large room, [there were] all the coal scuttles to carry and I used to have to clean on my hands and knees from the front door right through to the back. Then whitened the front door step every morning. Oh, it was hard in them days, and at Christmas Mrs. Learmonth used to have us all in after lunch .. We all had to stand in a line right along the hall then go up to the spare room or sitting room ... and receive our presents ... she had all these presents and gave the under servants, me and the kitchen maid a black piece of material, not a dress, a piece of material to make a dress!

Edith Blackman also left a fascinating account of her childhood in a cottage opposite the Purbrook Industrial School at Stakes in the early 1890s.

> On Saturdays our kitchen always had an extra clean up. The stove was black-leaded and shone. The floor was a brick one but was covered with close-woven sacking which grandmother used to give us every year. She got it from Gale's brewery. I think it was what the hops came in ... It covered the floor and had only one seam up the middle. It was hemmed round the edge ...
> We all wore boots in those days. Shoes were worn only by the better off folks. When we wanted a new pair of boots Mother took the measurement with a piece of string on the sole of our boots. She wrote a little note and gave it to the Carrier who went to Portsmouth. He took it to the shoe shop and brought back two or three pairs for us to try on. Then called next day and took the unwanted ones back and the money for the pair we kept. Smith and Dacombe were carriers from Waterlooville and they came around Stakes on certain days. Their charge was very small 3d or 6d. They also used to get a cask of beer for father.
> A man used to come from Portsmouth carrying a big basket sometimes on his arm and othertimes on his head. He was selling laces, buttons, tapes, combs, kettle-holders, cake tins, tin plates and all such things. We used to call him the Mistress Man because he used to say as we opened the door 'Now Mistress, what can I do you today'. It was handy as one had to go a mile to get these odds and ends.
> There was a little shop in Stakes about ten minutes walk away from us. It was a post office and sold sweets and odd things in groceries such as sugar, flour, biscuits and tobacco. The main part of our groceries came from Pinks at Portsmouth. Mother sent an order every Friday by post. We often had to run at the last minute to catch the post on Saturday. It was a big parcel. We all came around Mother to see if there was anything to eat. Sometimes she would put some cocoa and sugar on a bit of paper and we played teas—or a few currants or some coconut—but only a little. Mother used to buy breasts of lamb and bone and stuff them and this was our Sunday joint.

While considerable change occurred in most aspects of life in the 20th century conditions for servants changed little, for in the 1920s Elsie Leach earned five shillings a week and had to buy her morning and afternoon uniforms out of her wages, attend church twice every Sunday and got a half day off each fortnight. In the early 1930s she went to work for the Gurnell family, newsagents and stationers in London Road, at Swiss Cottage (now the Citizens' Advice Bureau) as maid of all work. She was responsible for the cleaning and laundry of the whole house (a family of four) for eight shillings all found. At least building workers were better paid. At Edwards, at the beginning of the century, the highest paid worker, the foreman, received £1 15s. for a 60-hour working week. The lowest paid worker received 15s. with only marginal increases occurring before the First World War. Clearly the lives of those who did menial tasks were a world apart from those of the wealthy and those who flourished in business.

Among the latter in the 19th century were Thomas and Elizabeth Nichols, whose Waterloo Laundry was established in 1886 and from where vans from Southsea collected four days a week; William Alfred Hall, a timber merchant, of Stakes Hill Road in the 1880s who moved to Mill Hill where, despite his windmill being destroyed by fire in the early years of the 20th century, he was subsequently able to expand his steam mills; and the Wadham Brothers.

In June 1900 Edwards Builders put a window in Harold Wadham's cycle shop, and in January 1905 Edwards built him a workshop in Stakes Hill Road for £19 15s. 3d., from which his motor business was to begin and where he was joined by his brother, Wilfred, that same year. This was underneath the Victoria Hall, but their stay there was relatively short, ending dramatically in 1907 as Harold carelessly struck a match when inspecting the gearbox of a Peugeot, below which was a bath of petrol. Harold managed to get the car outside and the fire brigade, located close by, behind the *Heroes*, soon arrived but, unaccustomed to petrol fires, their hose soon had a river of burning petrol flowing down Stakes Hill Road. Two cars and two dozen bicycles were destroyed in the blaze. The following year Wadham's opened a showroom in new premises, built by Edwards, in London Road north-east of the *Heroes* and workshops in Hambledon Road behind the hotel. From there, although they retained an interest in cycles, Wadham Brothers were to expand into the new world of automobiles. But perhaps, for the purpose of this book, the most important arrival as a successful businessman was C.H.T. Marshall. Brought up at Stakes, where his widowed mother became sub-postmistress from the 1890s, Herbert Marshall was a progressive and ingenious photographer recording many scenes of Waterlooville life in the early 20th century. He would have preferred to have been an engineer and many of his photographs indicate this, especially those of the building of the Portsdown and Horndean Light Railway. Construction began from Cosham in January 1902 and it was complete to Horndean, through Waterlooville, in March 1903, services commencing on 3 March.

The opening of this line, with its emerald green and cream trams, was both to contribute substantially to the growth of Waterlooville and also to confirm the attraction of the area for visitors in the early 20th century, a 10-minute service being maintained in the late spring, summer and autumn.

Waterlooville was then described as: 'A very modern and up to date village, the residence of many influential Portsmouth people ... The shops also will bear comparison with those in much larger towns ... and everything may be obtained at town prices, and of standard quality'. Concerts were given both in the Victoria Hall and, from 1912, in St George's Hall when it was built by Edwards to the west of the church. The village also had: 'a well fitted and commodious reading room possessing besides a library, a bagatelle table and other means of recreation, at the rear of these premises is situated a well patronised Rifle Club of nearly 100 members'. A Choral Society was established in 1902 and the Cricket Club was well known with a ground not far into the north side of Hulbert Road, lying in the midst of beautiful surroundings where the Waterlooville Annual Flower Show was also held. Waterlooville Football Club was formed in 1905 playing at the recreation ground in the Waterlooville & District League until just before the Second World War.

Thus, although a small village, it had developed considerable opportunities for sport and leisure, including many pleasant rural walks. Perhaps one of the residents' favourites was to walk a third of a mile down Stakes Hill Road where, on the north side, was a white swing gate opening into the popular Lovers Walk which led across the New Road (Hulbert Road) into Bere Forest (Hurstwood) on a broad path which, bearing to the left, went to Highfield House and then back to the London Road, or bearing right it was possible to walk to Cowplain or Horndean. A mile along Stakes Hill Road was Stakes:

> a very healthy locality [with] pretty country villas ... [and] residences are much sought after ... . No better summer evening's stroll could be had from Waterlooville ... by way of Stakes Hill to Purbrook, or through the woods when the nightingales are in full song, and the odour of pines everywhere.

Waterlooville in the early 20th century was clearly a delightful place and these descriptions (*William's Guide* 1910) are borne out by so many of Herbert Marshall's photographs. However, increasing traffic would certainly bring changes. In 1911 the Parish Council requested the County Council to provide a footpath from Hambledon Road to Wallis Road, as the other side of the road from Hulbert Road north-east was used by the light railway. The council also stated that they would take up their duties regarding lighting of roads with gas. The footpath, however, was still in a bad state in January 1916 caused by the introduction of underground telegraph wires and the trench being unsatisfactorily refilled. Telephone wires were usually above ground, as photographs show, and had certainly been connected to Waterlooville and Stakes post offices by 1907 as well as some of the major businesses.

The onset of the First World War was to bring further changes. Edwards lost two thirds of their workers to the forces; of 33 men in 1913 only 11 remained in December 1914. All those paid at the lower end of the scale had gone, young labourers and apprentices—only the older men were left. Wadham's became a munitions factory and repairers of government vehicles, and three years of U-boat attacks brought a developing food crisis. Appointed local engineers for the Ministry of Food, they employed a number of Fordson tractors with troops involved in the ploughing which went on through the night. In January 1917 the Parish Council requested the inhabitants to 'cultivate the whole of the land at their disposal for the production of food'—32 cwts. of seed potatoes were distributed at 14s. 4d. per cwt. Major landowners were asked to provide allotments, resulting in the development of land on the north side of Winifred Road. Other aspects of war came with the conversion of St George's church hall into a Red Cross Hospital for the injured, and, tragically, the war was to see the premature end of many young men's lives and sadness for many local families. The rich and wealthy were not exempt from tragedy for Walter Hulbert, who had taken over Stakes Hill Lodge at the death of his father in 1908, was to lose his only son, George, who was killed only 14 days before the Armistice of 1918.

Unlike many communities, Waterlooville did not erect a war memorial but installed a memorial arch as an entrance to St George's churchyard and a memorial clock in the tower of the Baptist church. The Parish Council proposed a public meeting to discuss ways of celebrating the peace but only four residents attended. It was decided that the Flower Show, arranged for 19 and 20 August 1919, would also be the venue for peace festivities—perhaps the village was war weary. The war to end all wars was over and people wished to return to a normal life.

Not all aspects remained unchanged. The shortage of labour in the war, as men left for the forces, meant wages began to rise and those soldiers fortunate enough to return found themselves better paid than before the war. By 1920 Edwards Builders' staff numbers had risen from eight at the end of the war to 19, and their weekly pay ranged between £5 and £2 5s., increases of up to 200 per cent, except for apprentices who still received 16s. In many ways, however, it was a return to normal in inter-war Waterlooville. It was still the age of personal service with milk delivered in large pails suspended from a yoke and ladled out in half pint, pint or quart measures into customers' jugs, the pedlar who, from a large basket sold plates, including tin ones for children with the alphabet on the rim, and elderly Cockle Annie who walked with fresh cockles and fish from Emsworth to Stakes pushing pram wheels with a large tray covered in a white cloth.

These colourful characters were, however, the last of their kind—once they ceased to trade there were no similar replacements partly because, by the inter-war period, Waterlooville was a village of long-established businesses. Blackman's grocery store had started when the Hulbert Road was being constructed in the late 1870s and the workmen helped them by buying their foodstuffs, with Mrs. Blackman cooking their hams on her old open fire. They sold everything from groceries, tools and toys, hanging brushes and all things not affected by the weather outside. On the other side of the Stakes Hill Road junction was Wadham's successful drapery store, established in the 1860s, and Rix's ironmongery. Across the London Road Pook's printer's, stationer's and post office had been there since the first years of the century, as had Gurnell's stationer's and newsagent's, Wadham Brothers' motor showroom, which was extended in 1920, and Edwards Builders, who had been successfully trading longer than any of them. Their businesses were helped by the steady expansion of the village. The war had been one for 'heroes' and the government intended that those returning from the slaughter of the Somme and other battles would have 'homes fit for heroes to live in'. The Parish Council applied for a dozen of these workmen's cottages to be built in December 1918 and Edwards benefited from the 1919 and 1924 Housing Schemes which saw the development of Forest End.

Although much horse-drawn traffic was still to be seen as well as the occasional steam wagon, public transport had been well established by the trams which ran down the centre of the main road. However, with an increasing number of petrol-driven lorries, vans and cars, alighting from the trams in the centre of the road was becoming increasingly hazardous. As early as the summer of 1919 the Parish Council voiced its concern about 'the speed of motor cars passing through the village which was dangerous to other users of the road and that accidents have occurred thereby'.

A letter was written to Hampshire County Council requesting a speed limit of 10 m.p.h.! Further protests were made about the speed of motorists in 1925, 1926 and 1929. Eventually, in 1931, white lines (although not stop signs) were painted across the Hambledon and Stakes Hill Road junctions. A further bone of contention was the ditch by the footpath along the London Road between Queen's Road and the village. For some years the council had requested that piping be installed, as in some places the ditch was two feet deep and dangerous. The reply which eventually arrived from the County Surveyor in 1926 that 'because of the miners' lock out they had not been able to carry out the piping of ditches from Queen's Road to Waterlooville' must have been met with utter disbelief by the Parish Council, particularly as the work still had not been carried out in 1928! Whether it had been before the final meeting of the council in March 1932, when it was replaced by the Havant and Waterloo Urban District Council, is unknown. The other matter on which the local council spent much of its time was the provision of a recreation ground, especially from January 1925 when land with a pavilion, between Wallis and Park Roads, was given to the Parish Council. They voted to raise £1,000 to finance the layout of four tennis courts, a bowling green and a cricket field on 12 acres and, although running out of money in 1926, they did complete the task. Another facility was thus provided for the growing community, as was the case when the Roman Catholic Church of the Sacred Heart was constructed in 1923.

The 1930s saw the extension of the council housing at Forest End and, at last, the filling in of the northern quadrant of the village, when Dorset Buildings plus additional shops were erected next to the extended Wadham premises (see map 5). Opposite these came a new form of entertainment, the Curzon Cinema south of the Reading Room. But they also saw the filling in of the tram lines in the main street. For, on 3 October 1934, the last tram was run—the Portsdown and Horndean Light Railway was no more, having been bought out by the Southdown Bus Company. Similarly, Tanner's Denmead Queen buses, which had run to Waterlooville, were also acquired by Southdown. In a decade of depression it was important that new jobs could be provided, as they were by the arrival of Osmond and Osmond, initially manufacturers of leather goods, located at the rear of the northern side of Stakes Hill Road.

There also came the end of the historic division of Waterloo into two parishes, for the new Urban District Council at last saw Waterlooville formed into a single authority. Coincidental was the building of a secondary school at Hartplain. Thus for the first time older Waterlooville pupils were separated from the elementary school at the age of eleven. Changes also occurred at Stakes Hill Lodge with the first of the Hulbert family's female succession. This was shortly followed by their sale of the Stakes Hill Road Model Farm and its lands, opening the way for new development on the south side of the village—Warfield Avenue and Crescent being laid out on the north side of Stakes Hill Road and Elmwood and Beechwood Avenues began as a development on the south side (see map 6).

Even so, before the Second World War the village's eastern periphery was still covered by dense woods and its west by fields of grass or grain (see map 5). The highlight of the year in the inter-war period seems to have been the annual two-day Flower Show and Fair, held on the cricket field in Hulbert Road. Apart from the competitions for garden produce and the sports of obstacle races and tug-of-war, there were military bands and massive steam tractor engines bringing caravans and wagons of equipment for the steam-driven roundabouts, swing boats and chair-o-planes. Hoop-la, roll-a-penny stalls and other sideshows such as coconut shies and shooting galleries were ever present. The loud martial music would attract visitors to the fair in the evenings when, with no street lighting in Hulbert Road, the lights of the roundabouts and stalls would illuminate the whole area, which was filled with the laughter and squeals of those riding on the amusements with a mixture of joy and apprehension.

It was still a peaceful and tranquil community, but not for long. The September sunshine of 1939 was the last to be enjoyed for some years, and for some the last ever, as the world was plunged into war and the village became a hive of war-time activity with men garrisoned within and around for the duration. Emergency water supplies were investigated with old wells being examined for suitability and static water tanks located in the streets in case of fire-fighting requirements. Those not volunteering or conscripted were left to undertake air-raid precautions, civil defence and Home Guard duties, but Waterlooville was fortunate, apart from some shattered windows, to escape the bombs and mines which rained down on Portsmouth. Many, driven out of the city, fled over Portsdown Hill to be given refuge on floors or wherever sleep could be obtained—30 refugees were accommodated around the house and stables of Stakes Hill Lodge. Many young men left for armed service immediately—Wadham's lost 200 employees in September 1939 alone, and found their works changed entirely to war production. Food and clothing were rationed and gas masks had to be carried every-where—even by children to school. All the ornamental metal garden railings and gates were removed for the war effort.

Victoria Hall was a canteen for soldiers and St George's Hall and Waterloo Hall used for their dances, especially after the ordeal of Dunkirk. But it was at the time of Operation Overlord, the proposed D-Day landings, that the whole area was saturated with forces, the Queen's Enclosure being full of hundreds of soldiers with army trucks parked along the roadside under the trees, from Waterlooville to Horndean, and Army Camp A7 was set up around Stakes Hill Lodge—5,000 troops of differing nationalities. One night shortly before D Day all these men and their vehicles departed in total secrecy leaving thank you messages by the roadside.

The end of the war brought no immediate change to Waterlooville residents, rationing continued, and the process of rehabilitation was slow. Building licences were restricted and raw materials were scarce. The general state of repair of buildings which had deteriorated in war time declined further, so that a general air of dilapidation and shabbiness was inevitable; even the last grand house in the village centre, Melton House, was gradually falling into ruin by weather and neglect.

The exploits of the Football Club, however, brought some light to the village. Having joined the Portsmouth League in the season before the war they immediately won the third division and after the war followed this in 1946-7 by becoming second division champions, and then in three successive years, 1949-52, were first division champions. They immediately joined the Hampshire League gaining promotion to Division Two in their first season. The following year, 1954, they moved to their present ground at Jubilee Park and in that same year the first new shop since the war was opened in the village.

Shortly afterwards Waterlooville began to change beyond recognition. In 1910 the *William's Guide* had said of travelling along the Hambledon Road, that 'on the right the

Hart Plain Estate is rapidly developing as a building site'. Such development had remained limited to Hambledon Road and the beginning of Milton Road. But with the disappearance of the old Hart Plain House came the Berg Estate of 1,100 dwellings, mostly bungalows, begun in 1958 and filling in to the north of Waterlooville. However, this was only the beginning. The 1960s were to see an orgy of building both in and around the village. Between Hulbert Road and the London Road, in the north east, Highfield House was replaced by the Highfield Estate. In the early 1960s Frank's Coppice was sold for development by the Stakes Hill Lodge estate, resulting in the Hurstville Drive development—the popular ramble through Lovers Walk and the woods to Highfield or Horndean was no more. On the opposite side of the Stakes Hill Road further expansion took place south of both Beechwood Avenue and Broadlands mansion.

Although many of the new arrivals, in the age of the motor car, were commuters to Portsmouth, jobs had to be provided for others. Thus a new industrial estate was developed on the north side of Hambledon Road with some twenty new premises being built by 1966. Perhaps the most notable of the new businesses represented the growing affluence and leisure time for increasing numbers of the population. For in 1963, Dennis Rayner established Westerly Marine Construction, a company which successfully gained the Queen's Award for Export in 1969, 1970 and 1977. However, the rising pound in the early 1980s brought a collapse of exports and financial difficulties from which the company was rescued by Centreway Industries. Even so, in the first 25 years Westerly produced over 11,000 sailboats. Another leisure business arriving was Quick's archery specialists, who shared premises with Osmond and Osmond.

Meanwhile, Wadham Brothers were finding their premises in the London and Hambledon Roads too cramped as the demands for motoring increased. Thus they moved to much enlarged new premises in 1962-3 along the north frontage of Hambledon Road. They had, from the second decade of the century, been involved in building bodies on car chassis and had expanded into vans, lorries, coaches and, in 1932, ambulances, the first fibre-glass ambulance body being produced in 1958 and becoming a major seller in the 1960s. Vacating their premises in the centre of Waterlooville gave alternative possibilities for development on the site.

Changes in the village were to be no less considerable than in the surrounding fields and woods, and were perhaps presaged by the closure of the Curzon Cinema in 1959, a victim of the growth of television in the majority of homes. In the early 1960s a shopping precinct, Woolworth's, Boots and Tesco all appeared on the north-east side of London road—Melton House, Tuffland Lodge and the old shops were swept away. The incomplete precinct was later to be finished by the addition of the County Library and a public house. In 1966 on the other side of London Road, the old *Heroes* and the former Wadham's buildings were demolished to made way for the £600,000 Wellington precinct intended to contain 40 shops and a supermarket. A new *Heroes* pub was opened in the former doctor's house to the north of the shopping centre. Later the same year the most imposing piece of the village centre's architecture, the Baptist Chapel, was demolished. Much of the change was in the name of road widening as well as modernisation, but even in 1966 plans were already in hand to divert the A3 via a by-pass skirting the centre of what by now had become a town, thus making it completely free of through traffic and, in the process, road widening less necessary.

Meanwhile Wadham Brothers, having expanded into their new site, amalgamated in 1968 with Stringer Motors of Wiltshire to create Wadham Stringer Ltd., then in

Map VI Waterlooville and Stakes, 1939.

1979 became part of Tozer, Kemsley & Milbourn (TKM). Subsequently, they were integrated with Kennings to form the Wadham Kenning Motor Group. TKM became a large international company and in 1992 was acquired by Inchcape plc., thus Wadham Kenning is now part of Inchcape Motors International. At the time of the Inchcape takeover the coachbuilding side was separated and operates independently as WS (Coachbuilders), thus still retaining a Wadham connection and the services of many skilled local craftsmen.

On the sporting side the Football Club's consistent performances in the Hampshire League won them promotion to the Southern League in 1971, becoming Division One (South) champions in their first year.

As if all this growth and change were not enough, the local authority, long having had an interest in acquiring the Stakes Hill Lodge estate, did just that in January 1973, when most of it was bought for the colossal sum of £5.74 million, opening the way for further development on the acquired land. The house itself was destroyed by fire the following June. The small community of Stakes, which for centuries had been encompassed by woodland and remained a pleasant rural backwater, now became totally engulfed by development. By 1977 compulsory purchase orders for land on the line of the A3M had been issued and its subsequent building at least diverted through traffic from Waterlooville, essential in view of the lengthening queues which were beginning to affect the town centre. But in its wake came the filling in with housing of the rest of the woodland between the Highfield estate and the motorway. Sadly the area, which had few buildings of historic merit, was losing the one it had. In the early 1980s Broadlands was demolished for a DIY store and Berry Cottage, a listed building, for the new post office. Along the south-west side of Hambledon Road, Brambles Farm became another industrial estate from 1989, with a leisure centre and swimming pool which opened in 1991. The old Swiss and Portland Roads disappeared for a supermarket.

All was change and at the end of it little of the original Waterlooville was recognisable. The attractive community of Herbert Marshall's photographs had been lost forever and in its place flat-topped featureless concrete cubes were raised. From what was clearly a village which was a magnet to visitors, Waterlooville had become a town which was probably one of the least photogenic in Hampshire. Not surprisingly, therefore, as the 20th century nears its close there are few photographs of the town, except those which occur in local newspapers showing, from the air, acre upon acre of development.

Only the eastern quadrant of Waterlooville has land on which development is possible and, not surprisingly, plans are already in hand for major growth. Similarly, another shopping development on the former site of Osmond and Osmond and the old Board School and adjacent houses—mostly demolished in 1995—is planned. When all these are complete there will be little if any new land available and perhaps the 21st century will see Waterlooville pause for breath and at last cease to be one of Britain's most rapidly growing communities. But will there be much from the 20th century that the late 21st century will wish to preserve?

Waterlooville

1 Waterlooville in the 1890s, looking north from Mill Hill with the church tower on the left. The road is chalk and flint and the telegraph pole has only two telephone wires.

2 General view of the village about 1905 surrounded by trees and fields. Wait Lane End Farm is in the foreground.

3 *Left*. Looking north to the cross-roads in 1901 with the *Queen's Hotel*, built by Edwards in the 1880s, on the extreme left. It was a residential hotel frequented mainly by Portsmouth people wanting a holiday in the country. The building to its right still exists as a newsagent's. Note the trees in the centre of the village. A large beech tree blocks the view of the Baptist Church with a monkey puzzle to its left.

4 *Below left*. A similar view, again in 1901, showing Purnell's chemist's next to the newsagent's. The three-horse bus had come from Cosham and a group wait for it outside the *Heroes*. On the right, traps to Denmead are for hire. The cross-roads at the centre of the village is dominated by trees.

5 *Below*. London Road looking south in 1901. Note that the *Heroes* had been renamed the *Waterloo Hotel* and outside it there was no pavement. Opposite were only three shops north of the cross-roads and a three-horse bus is arriving from Cosham.

6 *Above left*. Portland Road in 1906 taken from the church. Swiss Cottage (now the Citizens' Advice Bureau) is on the right. Note the background is entirely of trees. Now the entrance to Asda is at the end of the road where the cottage is with the horse in front.

7 *Above*. Highfield Cottages, London Road on the way to Cowplain. Where the white gate stands is now the entrance to Highfield Road and in the foreground is the entrance to what is now Wallis Road.

8 *Left*. Waterlooville from about Mill Road with the newly arrived Portsdown and Horndean Light Railway—possibly the heaps of gravel by the roadside were left from the track laying.

9   London Road looking north in the early 1900s showing the *Wellington Inn* and *Queen's Hotel*, both owned by R.J. Scott. The large beech tree which previously blocked the view of the Baptist Church has already disappeared. The road, except for the tram line area, is still chalk and flint.

10   London Road, 1905, looking north towards the cross-roads where a tram awaits.

11 London Road looking south, from north of the cross-roads. On the left one house has had an extension built in the front garden to create a shop. The double tram lines outside the *Heroes* were for the cars to pass.

12 London Road looking north to the cross-roads. On the right Reader's delivery cart stands outside his Supply Stores. On the corner is the awning for Wadham's drapery store. Beyond the cross-roads is Blackman's Village Stores plus two more shops, and beyond is a whole street of private houses and gardens.

13 A green car outside the private houses north of the cross-roads. The imposing house on the left is Melton House, home of George Lancaster, the Baptist Church benefactor, and later of Vice-Admiral Leggett. The tram is approximately outside where Boots the chemist's is today.

14 London Road looking south towards Waterlooville from north of Jubilee Road. Here the tram track was laid along the side of the road.

15 The reverse direction—looking north along London Road from Hulbert Road, the entrance to which can be seen in the right foreground. William Crockford, carrier, had a daily service from Havant from the 1890s and his four-wheeled waggon is seen approaching.

16 Stakes Hill Road, looking west towards the cross-roads about 1905, a very rural scene. Warfield Avenue is now in the dip on the right.

17 Hambledon Hunt coming down Stakes Hill Road from the cross-roads about 1905. Already they have reached the end of the developed area.

18 At the end of the road before Stakes was the turning on the left into Lovers Walk which led to the Hulbert Road. From there it was possible to walk through the Hurst and Hazleton Woods to Horndean. Lovers Walk was where Hurstville Drive and Lancaster Way now are. From the 1960s the Ferndale and Hazleton estates removed most of the rest of this popular country walk.

19 Hambledon Hunt at the cross-roads in Stakes Hill Road. The buildings provide interesting information. Across the main road on the left-hand corner of Hambledon Road is James Restall's grocery shop, established 1846, but it had been in Stakes Hill Road until sometime in the 1870s when it moved here and also became the post office. However, there is no evidence of the post office by this time. On the right, the first building, advertising Webbs Ales, is the *Bricklayer's Arms*. Beyond is the Victoria Hall with J.H. Wadham's cycle shop, opened in 1904, occupying the ground floor. This became Wadham Brothers in 1905 when the partnership with Wilfred Wadham was formed. Thus this photograph must be from 1904-5.

HAMBLEDON HOUNDS, WEST PACK !

20 Hambledon Hounds West Pack in London Road about 1910. Reader's has become the County Supply Stores sometime between 1903 and 1907. On the extreme right is Rix's ironmonger's and furnished apartments are advertised to let on the sign by the monkey puzzle tree in the garden on the left.

21 The cross-roads on a day of celebration looking into Stakes Hill Road. H.G. Wadham's drapery shop carries an advertisement for Dunlop tyres sold by Wadham Brothers' motor works, so it must have been taken after 1907. Behind the shop is the garage which contained Wadham's delivery vehicles and beyond that is Waterlooville post office advertising Stephen's ink. This is the original shop where James Restall began his grocery business in 1846, but at this time would seem to be in the hands of George Carswell Pook, who had taken over from his uncle as postmaster by 1903. Pook also ran a stationer's and printer's, hence the Stephen's ink advertisement.

22 An advertisement for Rix's ironmongery from the *William's Guide*, 1910. *See* picture 20.

IN THE CENTRE OF THE VILLAGE OF . . .

... WATERLOOVILLE,

— IS THE —

OLD-ESTABLISHED BUSINESS

— FOR —

Furnishing and General

IRONMONGERY

(ESTABLISHED 1860).

BRADE'S TOOLS.

THOS. TURNER & Co.'s CUTLERY.

All Kitchen and Domestic Requisites.

AMERICAN LAMP OILS.

CHINA AND GLASS.

Every kind of work done with promptness. Satisfaction guaranteed.

Plumbing.   Gas Fitting.   Electric Bells.

Alfred M. Rix.

NAT. TEL. **3 y,**

XX

23 Looking south from the cross-roads, *c*.1910. Horse traffic predominates.

WATERLOOVILLE

24 London Road looking north near Jubilee Road in 1908 showing the sylvan nature of its setting. The number 8 Green Car is advertising Knight and Lee, linen drapers.

25 London Road looking south showing the new Wadham Brothers' motor showroom built by Edwards in 1908 and representing the end of development on that side of the road. The motor works entrance was in Hambledon Road. The *Heroes* is hidden by trees.

26 London Road looking north towards the cross-roads at the end of the First World War in 1918—a rare photograph showing trams overtaking outside the *Heroes*, beyond which large trees still stand. Rix's ironmonger's has a galvanised tin bath hanging outside. Beyond, Harry Hoar's butcher's shop has become a bank.

27 The cross-roads looking south in 1922. The road is now surfaced and a pavement exists outside the *Heroes*. A workman is cleaning out the tram-line points at the beginning of the passing area. George Pook had moved his stationer's shop and post office to Restall's former grocery store once Restall had retired after over 60 years as a shopkeeper. His youngest son Lacey took over the Stakes Hill Road store for a few years after George Pook moved.

28 London Road looking north towards the cross-roads in 1928. Motor traffic has now replaced horse-drawn vehicles and an open-topped motor bus, advertising Landport Drapery Bazaar, now Allders, is competing with the trams for passengers.

29 London Road looking south, from south of the cross-roads in 1937. The monkey puzzle tree has gone, replaced by nurseryman Edward Francis's fruit and flower shop. The tram lines have been covered over and the poles which had supported the overhead wires now carry suspended street lights. The ironmonger's has even more goods hanging outside but is no longer Alfred Rix's—he had left in the early 1930s. In the background the road snakes up Mill Hill.

EDWARD FRANCIS,

WATERLOOVILLE.

Nurseryman, Seedsman & Florist,

HIGH-CLASS FRUITERER AND GREENGROCER.

❧ ❧ ❧

Garden Work of all description undertaken.

ALL KINDS OF BEDDING PLANTS IN SEASON.

Wreaths, Crosses and Bouquets a speciality.

CUT FLOWERS ALWAYS ON HAND

Nat. Tel. 1 x.

30 A 1910 advertisement for Francis's nursery.

31 Taken on the same day as picture 29, looking south from north of the cross-roads (note the loaded lorry parked on the left in the photograph is still there in the distance). Here the Waterloo Hall, a centre for dances, has been built where the *Heroes* tea garden was and adjoins Wadham's garlanded motor showroom. On its wall the Hall has an advertisement for new houses on sale for £595! The Hall was also an auction mart. Across the road the shops have extended from the three at the cross-roads and the nearest here is Gauntlett's. The National Provincial Bank has replaced Pook's stationer's and post office. The appearance of Belisha beacons reflects the increasing number of vehicles.

32 London Road a year later, taken from in front of the Curzon Cinema (now Curzon Rooms) with the entrance to Melton House seen where the sunshine comes through the trees. On the opposite side of the road Dorset Buildings with J.E. Smith's garage and coal merchant's nearer the camera, plus another four shops have extended the village beyond the Wadham's motor showroom.

33 London Road looking north towards the cross-roads in 1938 and showing more commercial development. Three of the houses in Wellington Terrace have had shops built in their gardens and across the road Dick Bond stands, hands on hips, outside his garage.

34 Also looking north but nearer the cross-roads. Rix's ironmonger's has become Uden's, and Pink's have replaced Lankester and Crook and the County Supply Stores. Lloyds Bank is between them and Wadham's on the corner. The Worlds Stores appear where a garden and house previously existed.

35 The following three photographs are said to belong to the 1930s. But if so, they could only be from 1939 as a keep-left bollard has appeared in the centre of the London Road at the cross-roads and a telephone kiosk in the corner by the Waterloo Hall since 1938.

36 A view from further north along the London Road showing more traffic. Dorset Buildings are next to Wadham's on the right.

37 Looking north towards the cross-roads. An enclosed double-decker bus is heading for Portsmouth and a second telephone kiosk has appeared on the right-hand pavement. A bustling commercial centre is indicated.

38 *Left*. General view of Waterlooville with cars climbing Mill Hill and Forest End in the foreground.

39 *Below*. A view from higher up Mill Hill, probably after the Second World War.

40 *Above*. London Road looking north to the junction with the Hulbert Road (B2150). Development has continued along the road including the dentist's house and next to it the doctor's, partly hidden, which is now the *Heroes of Waterloo*.

41 London Road looking towards the cross-roads in 1967. Already on the left is a space where the *Queen's Hotel* has been demolished. Square flat-topped blocks have replaced some original buildings on the right. The day following this photograph the attractive Baptist Church was demolished. It, and the *Queen's*, were replaced by concrete cubes.

42 London Road looking north towards the cross-roads in 1979. Little now remains of old Waterlooville, only the buildings on the right before the cross-roads and Rumbelows beyond (formerly Blackman's). All others have gone including, in the interests of road widening, the *Heroes*.

43 The site of Melton House became a shopping precinct. More flat-topped cubes with a covered walkway contrast with the 1930s buildings opposite, including Napper's, ironmongery and Sidney Slape's, fishmonger's. Isolated is the only tree left in the main street.

44 Berry Cottage, the offices of Edwards Builders, at the corner of Swiss Road and Hambledon Road and a listed building, was demolished to create space for the new post office.

45 Aerial photograph in 1985 showing northern part of London Road now precincted, with the new inner by-pass slicing through Hambledon Road. The largest building is the Asda supermarket which has replaced the rear half of Portland and Swiss Roads. Beyond is Forest End and then fields—the only undeveloped area—now under threat of development.

Stakes

46 The rural setting of Stakes about 1905; the post office is dimly seen across the field in the centre.

47 A closer view of Stakes post office about 1905. Herbert Marshall's mother was postmistress and after his marriage he lived in the adjoining cottage. No pavements exist although there is a street light.

48 A later photograph with the post office now at the end of the road. The postman delivers on the left where a proper footpath exists. Telegraph poles have appeared on the right.

49 Almost the same location, probably around 1910-20, after an unusually heavy snowfall. Even so, the bedroom windows are still wide open to freshen the air! Note the appearance of the telegraph pole.

50 A summer view of the same area a few years later, the telegraph pole showing three times as many telephone wires, and a post box has been installed in the wall of the post office just beyond the roadside window. Still no pavements provided. Today Philip Road is on the left just out of the photograph.

51 Stakes about 1920, with the postman walking back towards the post office. Here again the telegraph pole indicates the arrival of the telephone. The entrance to Oaklands is by the white railings and Oaklands Lodge can be faintly seen through the trees on the left.

Stakes Hill Road

M/W

52 *Left.* Another heavy snowfall but the telegraph poles indicate a later winter than that in photograph 49. This is Stakes Hill Road looking from Stakes to Waterlooville. Only a single house in the distance on the left of the road interrupts the rural scene.

53 *Below left.* The same view taken in summer some years later. The telegraph poles have been regularised on the right-hand side of the road. Other houses have appeared in the fields in the distance. The entrance to Lovers Walk is on the right and there are still no pavements for the ladies pushing their prams—but no traffic either.

54 *Below.* The entrance drive and Lodge House for Oaklands. Above the door the stone shield carries the words 'Ready Aye Ready'.

THE LODGE OAKLANDS. 32.

55 *Above*. Oaklands House, home of General Napier in the late 19th and early 20th centuries, and of Colonel Williams in the 1920s and 1930s; now converted into a secondary school.

56 *Right*. Oaklands Farm on the left looking north towards Stakes (Oaklands House is further along on the right). The farmhouse was the most southerly building in Stakes. The next further south was Purbrook Industrial School.

57 *Above right*. Rockville, home of the Learmonth family from the 1880s to about the First World War. Afterwards it had a number of owners until its demolition to make way for the building of Gloucester Road.

58 The last picture of the old *Fox and Hounds*, a favourite old country inn, about to be demolished. Behind it to the right can be seen the new *Fox and Hounds*. The cottage on the left of the old pub has already been demolished.

59 The site of the old *Fox and Hounds*, now part of the car park of the new one about 1930. The old post office is on the right and a bus stop sign has appeared on the left of Stakes Hill Road, but still no pavements.

Work

60 Agriculture was the most important economic activity in 19th-century Waterlooville. Here the hay harvest is being loaded onto the two-wheeled hay cart using a two-pronged hay fork.

61 Here the hay is being taken back to the farm to be made into ricks like those in the field on the right. An extra horse has been added to haul the load up the hill.

62 A trio of horses pulling an early mechanical reaper which replaced scythes in the late 19th century. A Marshall photograph taken near Waterlooville.

63 Shire horses, the real workhorses of the farms, were gradually replaced by tractors. These three splendid examples were photographed soon after the First World War at Highfield.

64 Workmen and their young assistants laying the track for the Portsdown and Horndean Light Railway outside the *Wellington Inn*. The foreman stands on the left, complete with jacket, waistcoat, collar and tie and watch. Behind him are the houses of Wellington Terrace. R.J. Scott stands in the doorway of his inn. A poster advertising a grand concert and a comical farce at the Victoria Hall is displayed in the window.

65 Tramway men who worked on the maintenance of the Light Railway. In this case the foreman, Jimmy Chace, wore a bowler hat.

66   After the Armistice, Mr. and Mrs. Read of Billett Avenue gave a celebratory Sunday morning breakfast at the village's *Queen's Hotel* for all the employees of the Light Railway. As only two trams ran on Sunday, employees could attend.

67 Edwards Builders' managers and staff after the completion of St George's Church Hall and Sunday School in 1912. The company is the oldest established in Waterlooville. Its founder John Edwards, seated with his dog in the centre, was an apprentice bricklayer in 1851, but had begun his own company by 1860. Here his son, John, sits two to his right, and his grandson, Frank, stands behind his right shoulder. Tony Edwards, his great grandson, now heads the company.

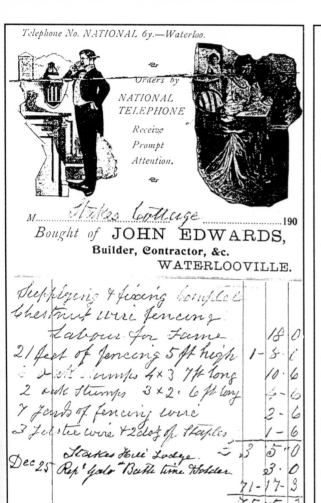

Telephone No. NATIONAL 6y.—Waterloo.

Orders by
NATIONAL
TELEPHONE
Receive
Prompt
Attention.

M. *Stokes Cottage* 190

Bought of JOHN EDWARDS,
Builder, Contractor, &c.
WATERLOOVILLE.

Supplying & fixing complete
Chestnut wire fencing.
    Labour for same   18 0
21 feet of fencing 5 ft high   1 8 0
  oak stumps 4 × 3 7 ft long   10 6
2 oak stumps 3 × 2. 6 ft long   6 6
7 yards of fencing wire   2 6
3 plain wire + 2 doz of staples   1 6
    Stakes Hill Lodge   3 5 0
Dec 25 Rep^d Galv^d Bath time holder   3 0
       71 17 3
       £5 15 3

Visitors to Waterlooville should not fail to visit

GEORGE C. POOK,

At the Post Office,

FOR

Local View Post Cards & Novelties

CIRCULATING LIBRARY (In connection with Mudie's)

STATIONER, BOOKSELLER & NEWSAGENT.

NATIONAL TELEPHONE

EDWARDS & SON,

(Established at Waterlooville over 50 years)

General and Furnishing Ironmongers,

Builders' Merchants, &c.

✤ ✤ ✤

Plumbing, Gas and Hot Water Fitting.

Electric Bells Repaired and Installed.

ESTIMATES FREE.

A. E. JEFFERY,

Practical Watchmaker & Jeweller,

MEDINA VILLAS, WATERLOOVILLE.

CLOCKS WOUND AND REPAIRED BY CONTRACT.

PHONOGRAPHS AND GRAMAPHONES REPAIRED.

All Work Guaranteed.   16 Years Experience.   Established 1901.

ix

68 *Above left.* An Edwards bill to the Hulberts for fencing and repairing a galvanised bath at Stakes Hill Lodge early this century.

69 *Above right.* A page of advertisements from the 1910 *William's Guide* including one for Edwards, as well as ones for Pook and Jeffery.

70 Waterlooville Mill during damping down after the fire which destroyed it. *William's Guide* (1910) states 'the old mill was destroyed by fire about three years ago', so this photograph was taken about 1907. Smoke still rises from timbers on the right, while staff empty buckets on the remains.

71 Waterlooville's first volunteer Fire Brigade about 1910 when the fire engine was housed at the rear of the *Heroes*. The photograph was taken in the tea garden.

WATERLOOVILLE FIRE BRIGADE (1)

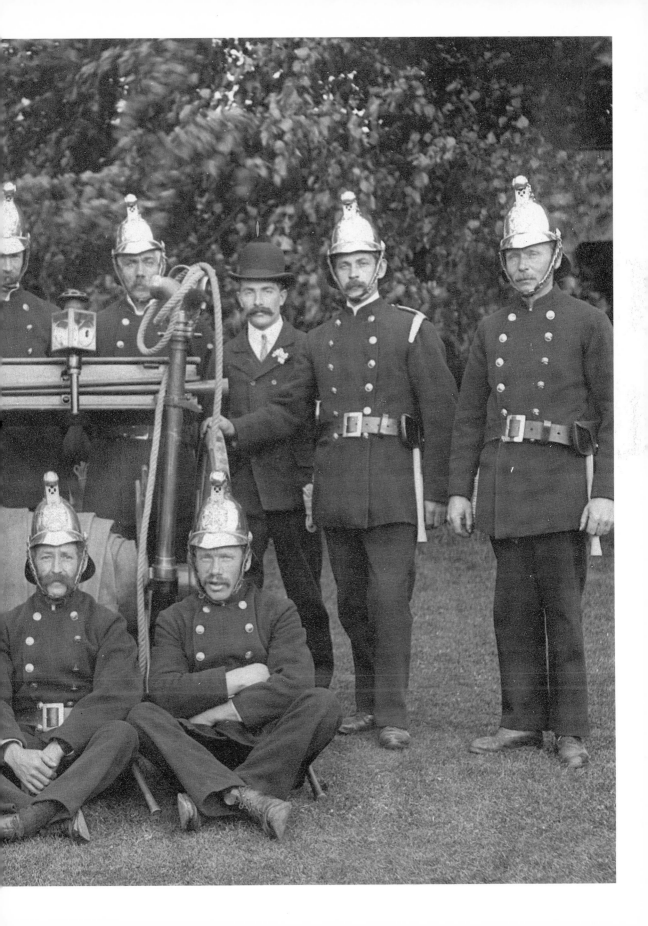

72 The Fire Brigade about the late 1920s or early 1930s, then organised by chief officer Jack Ganson, landlord of the *Heroes* from the late 1920s to the late 1930s. Ganson is sitting third from right. The uniforms, apart from the officers' peaked caps and the long leather boots, appear to be the same as those in the previous photograph.

73 Silver Jubilee celebrations, 1935. The Fire Brigade now has a motorised fire engine which came from Havant two years earlier, shortly after the formation of the Havant and Waterloo Urban District Council. Here it is seen in front of the *Queen's Hotel* and Gurnell's stationer's shop (still a newsagent's).

74 The new Merryweather 'Hatfield' fire engine delivered in 1937 and seen here in 1939 outside J.E. Smith, coal merchants, who leased their large garage in London Road as the Fire Brigade station.

75 Jack Ganson also raised money for an ambulance. The increasing number of vehicles meant more road accidents. The one purchased can be seen here alongside the fire engine opposite J.E. Smith's in London Road. The trees are probably in the garden of Melton House.

76 Wadham Brothers became Waterlooville's largest employers, but this is the original Hambledon Road workshop built by Edwards in 1908, with the workforce gathered outside. This photograph must be after 1912 when St George's Hall was built and before the building of the First World War Memorial Arch entrance to the churchyard. Thus this photograph must be between 1912 and 1920.

77 A corner of Wadham's machine shop during the Second World War. The Waterlooville works carried out advanced engineering for the Admiralty and the Air Force. Note that women workers had replaced many men.

78 The Civil Defence Unit of Waterlooville photographed in the garden of the *Heroes* in 1943. Note that almost all are ladies but their commander is male—Dr. Lennox Stevenson seated in the centre.

79 In 1930 Osmond and Osmond, basket and leather goods makers, came to Waterlooville located in the garden at the back of Mr. Osmond's house in Stakes Hill Road (the house was to the left of Wadham's first drapery store—see photograph number 81). Here the men, making a variety of dog and cat baskets and hampers from willow in 1958-9, are *left to right* Bert Marthouse, foreman, Jim Ware, Wally Brown, Arthur Weston (who still works at the company), Ron (Tommy) Weston, Albert Coles, Roy Weston, Bill Littlefield, and Sid Norman. The three Westons were brothers.

80 The leather workshop at Osmond and Osmond in 1958-9. Behind the screen on the left is Angela Holland (née Eames) and facing her on the bench outside is Kitty Horne. Sitting in the far corner, wearing a white top, is Jeanie Bates and on the far right using a Singer sewing machine is Mrs. Lower. Among those seated around the table in the centre are Marilyn Woods and Mrs. Small.

Commerce

81 Wadham's original drapery shop on the north side of Stakes Hill Road in the early 20th century shortly before it moved to the southern corner of the junction with the London Road, where it remained until the 1960s. The house on the left is Mr. Osmond's, whose works grew from a building in the back garden.

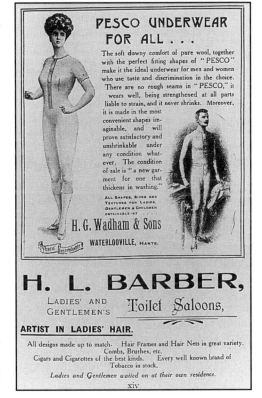

PESCO UNDERWEAR FOR ALL . . .

The soft downy comfort of pure wool, together with the perfect fitting shapes of " PESCO " make it the ideal underwear for men and women who use taste and discrimination in the choice. There are no rough seams in " PESCO," it wears well, being strengthened at all parts liable to strain, and it never shrinks. Moreover, it is made in the most convenient shapes imaginable, and will prove satisfactory and unshrinkable under any condition whatever. The condition of sale is " a new garment for one that thickens in washing."

ALL SHAPES, SIZES AND TEXTURES FOR LADIES, GENTLEMEN & CHILDREN OBTAINABLE AT . . .

H. G. Wadham & Sons

Pesco Unshrinkable WATERLOOVILLE, HANTS.

H. L. BARBER,
LADIES' AND GENTLEMEN'S
Toilet Saloons,

ARTIST IN LADIES' HAIR.

All designs made up to match.   Hair Frames and Hair Nets in great variety.
Combs, Brushes, etc.
Cigars and Cigarettes of the best kinds.   Every well known brand of Tobacco in stock.

Ladies and Gentlemen waited on at their own residence.

xiv

82 A 1910 advertisement for pure wool underwear obtainable at Wadham's, along with one for Barber's, hairdressers and tobacconists, who had the last shop on the London Road from the crossroads to Hulbert Road.

83 Charles Herbert Taylor Marshall, the Waterlooville photographer, about 1916 and without whom this book would not have been possible.

84 One of a series of shop signs which Marshall hung outside the old London Road studio.

85 The Marshall studio, probably in the late 1960s or early 1970s, stating that the business was established in 1901.

86 A 1910 advertisement for Marshall using only his initial H and showing that he took photographs in private homes. Below is an advertisement for Gurnell's, above which Marshall established his first studio.

H. MARSHALL, *Photographer,*

THE STUDIO, *Waterlooville.*

PORTRAITS AND GROUPS.
CUSTOMERS WAITED UPON AT THEIR OWN RESIDENCES.
CHILDREN'S PORTRAITS A SPECIALITY.

W. GURNELL,
Stationer, Newsagent and Printer,
CIRCULATING LIBRARY.
. . . NEWEST NOVELS AND BEST BOOKS.

SOLE AGENT FOR GOSS CHINA.
The Library, Waterlooville.

ESTABLISHED 1886.

T. & E. Nichols

Family Laundry,

SHIRT & COLLAR DRESSERS,

Waterloo Laundry,

WATERLOOVILLE.

—❖—❖—

AWARDED BRONZE MEDAL, LONDON, 1898.

—❖—❖—

Vans visit Southsea for collection and delivery four days weekly.

PRICE LIST ON APPLICATION.

iii

87 Nichols' Waterloo Laundry operated in the village for over 60 years on the site of the old Farlington Workhouse, now occupied by Asda.

88 Blackman's Village Stores, established in 1873, on the corner of Stakes Hill Road and the London Road. Bacon and brushes stand outside and were taken in every night after which it was difficult to move around the shop.

89 Martin's butchery in Stakes Hill Road with a display of poultry, pigs and meat, the scale of which suggests either much meat was eaten or the shop had been emptied for the photograph.

C. MEARS,

Family Butcher and Grazier,

LONDON ROAD,
WATERLOOVILLE.

Poultry, Rabbits, etc.

Fine Pickled Tongues and Corned Beef. . . .

. . . Sausages and Pork Fresh Daily.

ICE SUPPLIED IN ANY QUANTITIES.

Families waited on daily and supplied with Best Wether Mutton & Ox Beef.

NAT. TELEPHONE 2y.

X

90 Marsh's butcher's shop with a similar gigantic display of the wares, possibly at Christmas, since there is much poultry and some decorative holly. The photograph is from the 1920s, as indicated by the delivery van on the right. More local deliveries would no doubt be carried out by the young man with the bicycle on the left. The van states that Marsh's were also fishmongers.

91 Butchers' shops were clearly more prolific per head of population earlier this century. Here another London Road butcher advertises in 1910.

92 The following three photographs are inter-related, showing change in the centre of Waterlooville. The first pictures the *Heroes* in the process of demolition. To its right on the former site of the Waterloo Hall can just be seen Winter's builders merchants.

93 Winter's next to the now demolished *Heroes*. In its place a board advertises the new Wellington Way shopping precinct. The shop on the right is being fitted out.

94 *Above left.* Winter's on the left with the shop to the right now occupied by Bailey's florist's and beyond the Westminster Bank with Wadham's original motor showroom and their extension, with flag flying, further on. However, it was soon to go, replaced by the Wellington Way development. The reflection shows the Co-operative butcher's opposite.

95 *Left.* The demolition of the Wadham Brothers' showroom and works in the London and Hambledon Roads opened the way for the Wellington Way development. McIlroy's department store stands at the junction of the 'T' shaped precinct.

96 *Above.* McIlroy's staff adorn the Wellington Way cannon.

97 Wadham's moved further along the Hambledon Road, opening their new works and showroom at the foot of Red Hill. Here a winter's evening display of Minis adorns the much larger showroom.

98 Special Christmas display showing the old and the new. One of the coaches which could have been operating when Waterlooville began in the early 19th century is contrasted with an Austin/Morris 1100.

99 The interior of Christie-Nellthorp's hardware and DIY store on the London Road south of the cross-roads in the late 1960s or early 1970s. The modern equivalent of Rix's ironmonger's.

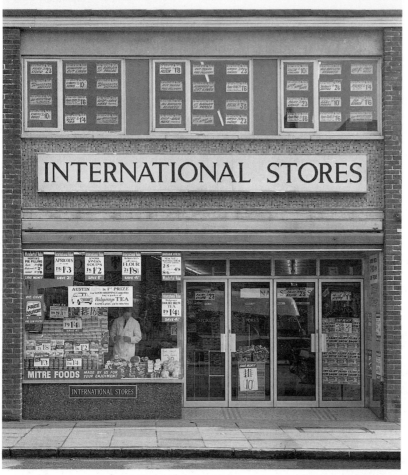

100 A modern grocer's shop, International Stores, was next door to Christie-Nellthorp's (to the left). Note the flat-roofed cubic building.

101 On the industrial estate on the north side of Hambledon Road, Westerly Marine boatbuilders, was a successful company from its foundation in 1963 to the early 1980s. Having weathered the recession, they still remain in Waterlooville.

Transport

102 Stagecoaches were replaced by railways for long distance travel in the 19th century, but railway stations had to be served by local transport and Waterlooville had its three horse buses to Cosham station. Here the staff of the Waterlooville depot, with two examples of the open-topped buses, are pictured in the stable yard behind the *Heroes*. Drivers, like Jimmy Goble on the right-hand bus, wore bowler hats; not to be confused with the bearded R.J. Scott in the centre, who was proprietor of the *Wellington Inn* and the *Queen's Hotel*, as well as, at one time, the *Good Intent*, Horndean.

A. J. COLLYER,

(Late J. SMITH)

Coal, Wood, & Oil Merchant,

WATERLOOVILLE.

Waterloo, Stakes, Purbrook, and Portsmouth Daily Carrier.

FURNITURE REMOVED.

NOTED FOR SEABORNE COALS.   *Estimates free.*

FAMILIES WAITED ON DAILY BY REQUEST.

Nat. Tel. No. 21 y.

103 Not only people but goods were carried by horse-drawn carriage. Here, outside James Smith's coal merchant and general carrier in Victoria Road, is the covered cart of A.J. Collyer who had replaced Smith. Pictured are Reginald and Kate Collyer with their father's horse and cart. They lived in Ebenezer Cottage, Victoria Road.

104 Collyer's advertisement in 1910. He was a fuel merchant and furniture remover as well as a daily carrier locally.

105 A double indicator of the new age of transport. First, the steam locomotive intended to transfer the success of the railways to roads, but only lasting for a short period. Secondly, the green cars of the Portsdown and Horndean Light Railway, here having stopped outside the *Queen's Hotel*. Note the staircase to the non-existent upper deck which would be coachbuilt at the Cowplain depot, to which these first tramcars were being delivered in 1902.

PORTSDOWN & HORNDEAN LIGHT RAILWAY.

——:o:——

Summer Service.

——:o:——

On and after Thursday, July 11th,

the Car Service will be re-arranged to work to the following times.

DOWN CARS FOR COSHAM LEAVE:

Horndean—8.0, 8.20, 8.40. 9.0, 9.20, 9.40, 10.0, 10.20, 10.40, 11.0 a.m., and every 10 minutes until 9.0 p.m., then 9.20, 9.40, 10.0, and 10.18.

Park Lane—7.50, 8.7, 8.27, 8.47, 9.7, 9.27, and every 10 minutes until 9.7 p.m., then 9.27, 9.47, 10.7, and 10.22.

Waterloo—7.55, 8.15, 8.35, 8.55, 9.15, 9.35, a.m. and every 10 minutes until 9.15 p.m., then 9.35, 9.55. 10.15 and 10.30.

— SUNDAYS. —

Horndean—10.10, 11.40, 1.0	and every 10 minutes as on week days—the last car being	10 p.m.
Park Lane—8.30, 10.17, 11.45, 1.7		10.7
Waterloo—8.35, 10.25, 11.50, 1.15		10.15

Purbrook—Depart 5 Minutes after Waterloo.

UP CARS FOR HORNDEAN LEAVE:

Cosham—8.30, 8.50, 9.10, 9.30, 9.50, 10.10 a.m., and every 10 minutes until 9.40 p.m.; then 9.50, 10.10, 10.30, 10.50. and 11.5.

Purbrook—Departure Times: 15 Minutes after Cosham.

Waterloo—8.55, 9.15, 9.35, 9.55, 10.15, 10.35 a.m., and every 10 minutes until 10.5 p.m., then 10.15, 10.35, 10.55. 11.15, and 11.25.

Park Lane—7.52, 8.12, 8.32, 8.52, 9.2, 9.22, 9.42, 10.2, 10.22. 10.42 a.m., and every 10 minutes until 10.12 p.m., the 10.22, 10.42, 11.2, 11.22, and 11.30 will only proceed if they have passengers for Horndean.

— SUNDAYS. —

Cosham—9.10, 11.5, 12.20, 1.50	and every 10 minutes as on week days—the last car being	10.50
Waterloo—9.35, 11.35, 12.40, 2.15		11.15
Park Lane—9.42, 11.32, 12.47, 2.22		—

——:o:——

J. FEREDAY GLENN, MANAGER.

xxv

PORTSDOWN & HORNDEAN LIGHT RAILWAY.

——:o:——

List of Revised Fares.

——:o:——

Cosham and the George Inn	**1d.**
George Inn and Purbrook (Leopard)	**1d.**
Purbrook (Leopard) **and Waterloo** (Hambledon Road)	**1d.**
Waterloo (Hambledon Road) **and Spotted Cow** (Cow Plain)	**1d.**
Park Lane (Car Shed) **and Horndean**	**1d.**
Cosham and Purbrook (Leopard)	**2d.**
George Inn and Waterloo (Hambledon Road) ...	**2d.**
Waterloo (Hambledon Road) **and Horndean** ...	**2d.**
Cosham and Waterloo (Hart Plain Siding) ...	**3d.**
Purbrook (Leopard) **and Horndean**	**3d.**
Cosham and Spotted Cow (Cow Plain)	**4d.**
Cosham and Horndean, single	**5d.**
Cosham and Horndean, return	**8d.**

The above returns are issued on any car throughout the day, and are available to return by any car the same day only; they are not transferable, and passengers cannot break and resume their journey with the same ticket.

——

Children under 12, one Penny for a 1d. or 2d. section, and Twopence for a 3d., 4d., or 5d. section.

School Tickets for Children under 16 years of age, available between 8 and 9.30 a.m., 12 and 2 p.m., and 4 and 6 p.m., as under:—

1d. Tickets (1s. a dozen) available for the full journey, to be had of the Inspector.

½d. Tickets, available in a 2d. section, issued on the cars.

Return Tickets are issued before 9.30 a.m.:

Cosham and Park Lane	4d.
Cosham and Horndean	6d.

J. FEREDAY GLENN,
MANAGER,
COSHAM, HANTS.

For Rates and Particulars of Special Cars apply to above address.

xxi

108 Yet another new form of transport, the motor car. This one is being refuelled outside Wadham Brothers' London Road showroom built in 1908. The photograph is dated 1909 and the hand-cranked petrol pump must have been a rare sight. The open space to the left was the *Heroes* tea garden.

109 The same building, probably at the same time, as the cars in the showroom have not changed and the one refuelled on the previous photograph is now behind the saloon by the petrol pump. On the *Heroes* side of the London Road the showroom was the last building, as indicated by the fields and trees on the right.

Telegrams:
"WADHAM.
Waterlooville."

'Phones—Offices. 38 Nat.
6 Corp.
Works, 38 a. 38 b, Nat
Residence. 3x.

Showroom:
LONDON ROAD.

Works:
HAMBLEDON RD.

WADHAM BROS.,

Automobile Engineers,

WATERLOOVILLE.

❧ ❧ ❧

We are the authorised Hants and W. Sussex Agents for the celebrated "Peugeot Automobiles"—the 1910 success of France."

Also sole district agents for the British-built 6-cylinder Standard.

We supply any make of car at the lowest possible prices, and will take your old car in part exchange.

Our works are the finest in the district, extending over 3,500 sq. feet, and only first-class mechanics, under direct supervision, are employed.

Our Hiring Department includes only first-class cars and chauffeurs.

Our Booklet and Tariff on application.

ii

110 A 1910 advertisement indicating the scale of Wadham Brothers' operation.

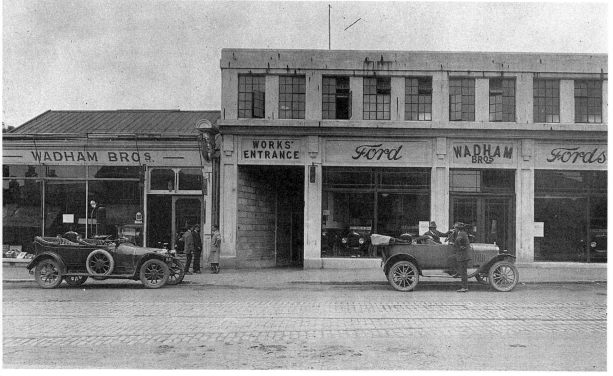

111 In 1919 Wadham Brothers had this large extension built on to their 1908 showroom. The works entrance went through to the coachbuilding workshops at the back which linked to the Hambledon Road building. In the same year they became Ford dealers.

112 The same year Wadham's completed an order for bodies on Thorneycroft buses for Portsmouth Corporation. Here, the open-topped buses are paraded outside the *Heroes* and its tea garden. Note the solid tyres and the name was still Corporation Tramways.

113 All the staff had to appear in this celebratory photograph. They numbered 50, with Wilfred and Harold Wadham sitting at each end of the driver's seat in the first bus. Note the open cabs for the drivers. The roof of Wadham's showroom is just visible above the fifth bus.

'Phone: WATERLOOVILLE 110.

SYMONDS BROS.

Motor Haulage Contractors.

5-TON and 2-TON LORRIES.

Distance no object

SPECIAL TERMS FOR CONTRACT WORK.

All kinds of Haulage Work Undertaken.

WATERLOOVILLE, HANTS.

114 An advertisement for Symonds motor haulage contractors from the early 1920s. The solid tyres must have given a bone shaking ride, as with the buses, but at least the cab was mostly enclosed against the weather.

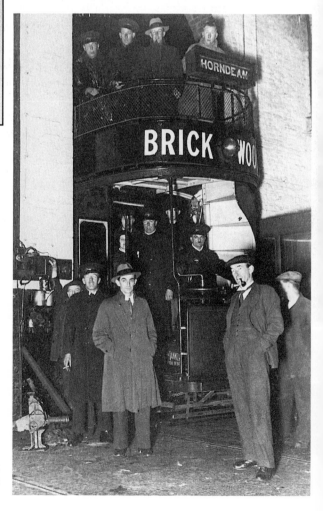

115 The last tram passed through Waterlooville on 3 October 1934, the Light Railway having been bought out by the Southdown Motor Company.

Text on vehicle: HAMBLEDON. — HAMBLEDON, DENMEAD, WATERLOO, TOWN HALL

116 The Denmead Queen buses were also bought out by Southdown from F.G. Tanner of Denmead. This early model was Wadham coachbuilt in the 1920s.

117 A Denmead Queen of the 1930s which ran regularly through Waterlooville to the Guildhall in Portsmouth and was the last of its line.

118 Apart from building bodies for cars, buses, vans and trucks, Wadham's began producing ambulance bodies in the inter-war period, building the first fleet of civilian-type ambulances supplied to the army. Here, in the new workshops in the late 1960s, is a new ambulance for Southampton Health Department.

Religion and Education

119 A 19-piece Waterloo School Band early this century dressed smartly for the camera. Note the severe haircuts no doubt partly to prevent infestation.

120 The original St George's Church about 1905 with the Sunday School on the left. Both have now gone, although one small part of the original church remains unseen behind the new building. Note the trees behind.

121 The memorial arch at the entrance to the churchyard, built in memory of all those Waterlooville residents who died for their country in the First World War.

122 Interior view of the original church—only the east end still remains.

123 St George's Church shortly before demolition. The original brick has been stone clad. Gravestones have been moved to the periphery of the churchyard and the buildings of the Wellington Way Precinct can now be seen behind.

124 A print of the original Waterloo Baptist Chapel built in 1856 in Chapel Lane. Note the trees of the Forest of Bere in the background.

125 The last years of the old chapel converted into a garage for panel beating, welding and respraying cars. Already, on the right, flat-topped buildings have been built in Hambledon Road and there are no visible trees.

126 The Italianate design of the Waterlooville Baptist Church and manse erected in 1884 and one of the village's most attractive buildings. The overhead wires of the Light Railway indicate that this is an early 20th-century photograph. On the left is the home of William Hawkes, cab proprietor, who hired out landaus, broughams, victorias, dog carts and brakes.

127 A later photograph, probably in the early 1930s (note the tram lines), showing that Campion's bakery had replaced Hawkes' house and garden.

Home and Leisure

128 Interior photographs from early this century are relatively rare; thus the following four Marshall ones taken about 1916 represent a tiny minority of those in this book. They were all taken at Marshall's Stakes cottage, next to the post office, and figure his wife, Ethel. In the first she is reading by the fireplace in the sitting/dining room on a spring day (note the daffodils). A coal fire burns in a black-leaded grate under a draped mantel shelf.

129 The wallpaper and tablecloth suggest that this is the opposite side of the same room with the table set for tea, and the Marshall's cat ready to partake.

130 The kitchen of the cottage, then with a modern gas cooker rather than cooking in an open fire, but has no hot water, only a cold tap is to be seen over a stoneware sink. The worktop is a table on which Ethel Marshall is making pastry.

131 In the bedroom, also having an open fireplace, is an iron bedstead with a linen bag hanging from it. The room is much lighter than the living room, with lighter wallpaper, furniture, fire surround and curtains.

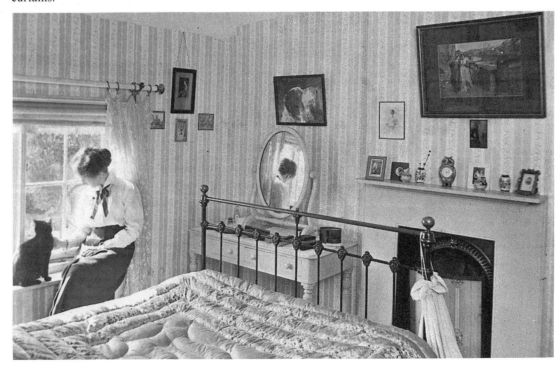

132 This photograph, taken on a day of celebration, has to be later than 1907 as Wadham's drapery shop has acquired new roller blinds since then (see photograph number 20, where the blinds are held up by poles on the pavement edge). Additionally, Reader's stores have become the County Supply Stores. Since Reader was still at his shop in 1907, this must be about 1910. A band leads the procession up the London Road.

133 The great event of the Waterlooville year was the Flower Show, held over two days in August on the cricket field in Hulbert Road. After the First World War, the parish council passed the organisation of the peace celebrations into the hands of the show committee. Clearly, these men (note no women) were regarded as very capable. The photograph shows the committee in 1908.

134 *Left*. Local veterans visiting the Flower Show in August 1931. From left to right are Councillor W.J. Over, Messrs D. Tarrant, C. Miles, W. Covell, D.A. Millett and H.S. Fielder. Their combined ages came to almost 500 years.

135 *Below*. Hunting was clearly popular in the early part of the century, but it also indicates how rural the area was about 1905. Here the hounds are coming up Red Hill, Hambledon Road with Red Hill cottages on the right, now the site of the by-pass, then all trees and fields. Those on the right are now covered by the industrial estate.

136 Waterlooville Rifle Club met at the back of the Reading Room. The team for 1908, shown here, was *back row*, G. Gardner, H. Ford, A. Budd; *second row*, G. Millett, C. Kiln, Mr. Saunders, H. Heath; *seated*, Mr. Millett, G. Miles, H. Marshall, Mr. Sparkes; *in front*, Mr. Barber, Mr. Olding and Mr. Sparkes.

137 Waterlooville Choral Society, formed in 1902, clearly offered a leisure activity for ladies. This undated photograph shows women outnumbering men by three to one.

GYMNASTIC DISPLAY AT WATERLOO (5)

138 In the early 20th century Waterlooville may have been a small village but was a community which pursued a remarkable number of activities. Here was another—a symmetrical display of gymnastics probably at the Flower Show in the Fairground (cricket) Field about 1912.

139 Waterlooville Football Club was formed in 1905 and this is their earliest photograph, taken at the Flower Show in 1908. By the players' dress, and especially that of the referee—masked and in a dressing gown—this was a light-hearted occasion, although the facial expressions do not support that view.

140 The team from the 1909-1910 season which competed in the Waterlooville and District League. They were known as the 'Pinks', not because of the colour of their shirts, but because they were largely formed from the staff of Pink's the grocer's.

141 After playing in the inter-war period in green shirts with a yellow 'v', the modern Waterlooville F.C. play in white with blue edging. This photograph is taken in front of the stand at the Jubilee Road ground.

142 The Parish Council established a recreation ground for the village, where for some time the Football Club played. Here dignitaries attend the opening ceremony in 1927.

143 The pubs of a village were often important social centres and meeting places. The oldest in Waterlooville was the *Heroes of Waterloo*. This splendid building was the second one to be built on the cross-roads site and is seen as a centre of activity on Hambledon Races day in 1905. James Restall's grocery shop is on the left and the trees of the *Heroes* tea garden on the right. The *Heroes* was demolished in 1965.

144 The *Wellington Inn* remains on its original site. This 1938 photograph shows the poplar trees in Chapel Lane on the right, and on the left is the billiard room, the Wellington Club room and, beyond, the houses of Wellington Terrace.

145 A rare photograph of the *Queen's Hotel* in the early 20th century. It was a residential temperance hotel and stood on the opposite side of Chapel Lane from the *Wellington*. The entrance to the tea garden at the rear is on the left.

146 The Curzon Cinema was built in the 1930s, but this photograph was taken shortly after its closure in 1959, victim of the growth of television. A hedge in front and trees on both sides indicate that, even as late as 1959, the village had rural features. The upper part is now the Curzon Rooms.

147 Wadham Brothers' children's Christmas and New Year party, 10 January 1953.

148 Probably a decade later but the same location and occasion. Some of these children may be now living in the area as adults with their own children, and their parents now grandparents.

Sources and Bibliography

Primary Sources

Hampshire Records Office
Q23/2/11/1-3 Bere Forest Enclosure Award, 1814 and map 1812
21M65/F7/89/1&2 Farlington Parish Tithe Award and map, 1838
69M84/PX1 Waterloo Parish Council Minute Book, 1911-32
15M74/DDB6 Miscellaneous Papers, 1939-43

Portsmouth City Records Office
CHU/45/1A/1 Waterlooville Parish Register, 1832-1908
CHU/45/2A/1 Vestry Minute Book, 1838-86
CHU/45/3/1-3 Act of Consecration, 1831
Ordnance Survey Maps: 1810 1 in.; 1895 6 in.; and 1939 25 in.

Hampshire Records Office and Portsmouth City Records Office
Censuses of Great Britain (copies of originals at PRO)

HO/107/390/5	1841
HO/107/1656	1851
RG/9/699	1861
RG/10/1219	1871
RG/11/1138	1881
RG/12/944 and 851	1891

Gales Brewery Archive—Title deeds of *Heroes of Waterloo*
Edwards Builders, Ledgers: 3 volumes: Vol. 1 1893-1905
                                        Vol. 2 1905-23
                                        Vol. 3 1923-34
                    Wages Book, 1900-21
A.G. Blackman, Scrapbook and Memoirs

Printed Sources

Trade Directories
Bennett's *Business Directory*: 1907
Directory of Hampshire: 1871
Kelly's *Directory of Hampshire*: 1859, 1880, 1885, 1889, 1895, 1903, 1907, 1911, 1923,
    1931, 1935, 1939
Kelly's *Post Office Directory of Hampshire*: 1867
Post Office *Directory of Hampshire*: 1855
White's *Directory of Hampshire*: 1859, 1878
William's Guide (1910)

Books

Harper, C.G., *The Portsmouth Road* (1928). A jaundiced view of Waterlooville.

Marshall, A., *Waterlooville—A Modern Village* (1983)

Newton, M. and Jackson, G.H.M., *The Rise and Fall of Stakes Hill Lodge 1899-1973* (1981)

Page, W. (ed.), *Victoria County History of Hampshire* (vols. 3 and 5, 1908-14)

Reger, A.J.C., *Waterlooville & District: Its History and Development* (1963)

Stapleton, B., *Hampshire of One Hundred Years Ago* (1993)

Todd, J.C., *William's Guide to some of the Beauty Spots on Portsdown & Horndean Light Railway* (1910)

Waterlooville, Farlington & Drayton—The Official Guide (n.d.)

Waterlooville Guide & Information Handbook (n.d., post 1974)

Articles and Pamphlets

Blackman, Edith, 'Childhood Memories' (unpublished) (1972)

Moorey, J., *Fifty Years of Service: The Story of Wadham Brothers 1905-1955* (n.d.)

Pile, J., 'Common-Pasture Exit Funnels and the Origin of Some Settlements in South-east Hampshire', *Hampshire Field Club and Archaeological Society, Section Newsletter*, New Series No. 23 (Spring 1995), pp. 19-26

Symons, E.T., *The House of Wadham Went to War* (n.d.)

Young, A.F., *The Founders of Wadham Brothers Motor Vehicle Distributors, Hampshire, 1905 onwards* (1982)

A Centenary History of Waterlooville Baptist Church (n.d.)

25 Years of Quality Boatbuilding—Westerly Yachts (n.d.)